"No family, not even a military one, is ever prepared for the holes that war and conflict punch ou⸱ ⸱ ⸱ ⸱⸱ ⸱⸱ ⸱⸱⸱⸱⸱⸱ ⸱⸱⸱⸱⸱. Waddell ⸱⸱⸱ ⸱ Orr's heartbreakingly beautiful ⸱⸱⸱⸱⸱ ⸱⸱⸱⸱⸱⸱⸱⸱ ⸱⸱⸱⸱⸱ ⸱ *Home*, is not only a personal ⸱ ⸱⸱⸱⸱⸱ ⸱⸱⸱⸱⸱ ⸱⸱⸱⸱⸱⸱ ⸱⸱⸱ ⸱ families go through, it is a gu⸱⸱⸱ ⸱⸱⸱⸱⸱⸱⸱ ⸱⸱⸱ ⸱⸱⸱⸱⸱ ⸱ must-read for anyone living wit⸱ ⸱⸱⸱⸱ ⸱⸱⸱⸱⸱⸱ ⸱⸱⸱⸱ ⸱⸱⸱⸱⸱⸱ traumatic stress disorder and traumatic brain injury."

—**Lee Woodruff**, author of *Those We Love Most*,
coauthor of the bestselling *In an Instant*,
contributing editor to *CBS This Morning*, and co-founder
of the Bob Woodruff Foundation (www.remind.org)

"Men and women returning from the front lines and those who support them from the home front face serious lifelong challenges in the aftermath of war. *Wounded Warrior, Wounded Home* provides knowledge, insight, support, and guidance to ease the adjustment experienced by all in the wake of combat. Waddell and Orr provide a resource that brings hope and healing to those who love, work, and live with our returning service members."

—**Roger Staubach**, Hall of Fame Dallas Cowboys quarterback,
Naval Academy graduate, and Vietnam veteran

"Military families are some of the greatest heroes of this generation. Unfortunately, their story of sacrifice is rarely told. Kelly and Marshéle have firsthand experience with the difficulties a military family goes through when a warrior returns home from the trauma of combat. Buy this book if you are a military family or want to know how you can support and encourage military families around you."

— **Jeff Struecker**, pastor, national speaker, and veteran whose
story is featured in the movie and book *Black Hawk Down*

"*Wounded Warrior, Wounded Home* is a story of courage and hope and healing. Its courage plunges us into the abyss of grief and sorrow, of loss and suffering, of anger and despair that is a daily reality for the soldier wounded by PTSD and TBI. But piercing through this darkness is a ray of hope; hope that the ocean of darkness can be overcome by the ocean of God's light and life, hope that it truly is possible to win out over compassion fatigue, hope that a new life-giving normal is attainable. And hope opens the door to healing; a healing that, while never perfect, is real and powerful and substantial. *Wounded Warrior, Wounded Home* is essential reading for all who love and are connected to the life and service of a combat veteran. For your sake, for your loved one's sake, get this book."

—**Dr. Richard J. Foster**, author of several books, including *Celebration of Discipline* and *Sanctuary of the Soul*, and founder of Renovaré Ministries International

"Challenges deeper than the physical wounds haunt the homes of our military families; these challenges are often unseen by the public. They are the invisible wounds of war. Military families, you are not alone on your journey. You are deserving of the help and hope given in *Wounded Warrior, Wounded Home*. You hold the key to adjusting to your new normal and living a positive and empowered life."

—**Tara E. Crooks**, co-founder of Army Wife Network and coauthor of *1001 Things to Love about Military Life*

"*Wounded Warrior, Wounded Home* is a book that everyone whose life is connected to a combat veteran should read. Through my work with military families, I have seen that there is hope to be found in the voices of real families living victoriously in the aftermath of war. This hope is what Marshéle Carter Waddell and Kelly K. Orr, PhD, bring to these noble families. The authors masterfully deal with the wounds of the present conflicts of PTSD and TBI by helping families navigate a road filled with unfamiliar dangers and a new kind of normal. I highly recommend this book to those in a military marriage and extended family members as well as churches, communities, and all who work with veterans of combat wars. The healing found in this book is the difference between life and death and is a must-read for anyone who loves a combat veteran."

—**Ellie Kay**, America's Military Family Expert™, bestselling author of *Heroes at Home*, international speaker, and media veteran

"Freedom from a darkness that has haunted for way too long! As the founder of a center that treats PTSD, I can personally tell you there are healing words of hope in these pages for you or a loved one."

—**Gregory L. Jantz**, PhD, C.E.D.S., founder of The Center for Counseling & Health Resources, Inc., and author of *Healing the Scars of Emotional Abuse*

Wounded Warrior, Wounded Home

Wounded Warrior, *Wounded Home*

Hope and Healing for Families Living with PTSD and TBI

Marshéle Carter Waddell and Kelly K. Orr, PhD, ABPP

Revell

a division of Baker Publishing Group
Grand Rapids, Michigan

Published by Revell
a division of Baker Publishing Group
P.O. Box 6287, Grand Rapids, MI 49516-6287
www.revellbooks.com

Printed in the United States of America

Library of Congress Cataloging-in-Publication Data
Waddell, Marshéle Carter.
    Wounded warrior, wounded home : hope and healing for families living with
PTSD and TBI / Marshéle Carter Waddell and Kelly K. Orr, PhD, ABPP.
      pages cm
    Includes bibliographical references.
    Summary: "The wife of a combat veteran and a licensed counselor help families
to cope and heal in the aftermath of a service member returning home with PTSD
and TBI"—Provided by publisher.
      ISBN 978-0-8007-2156-5 (pbk. : alk. paper))
      1. Post-traumatic stress disorder—Treatment—United States. 2. Brain damage—
Patients—Family relationships—United States. 3. Families of military personnel—
Mental health—United States. I. Orr, Kelly K. II. Title.
    RC552.P67W28 2013
    616.85′212—dc23   2012035796

The internet addresses, email addresses, and phone numbers in this book are accurate at the time of publication. They are provided as a resource. Baker Publishing Group does not endorse them or vouch for their content or permanence.

The information in this book is intended solely as an educational resource, not a tool to be used for medical diagnosis or treatment. The information presented is in no way a substitute for consultation with a personal health care professional. Readers should consult their personal health care professional before adopting any of the suggestions in this book or drawing inferences from the text. The authors and publisher specifically disclaim all responsibility for any liability, loss, or risk, personal or otherwise, which is incurred as a consequence, directly or indirectly, of the use of and/or application of any of the contents of this book.

In keeping with biblical principles of creation stewardship, Baker Publishing Group advocates the responsible use of our natural resources. As a member of the Green Press Initiative, our company uses recycled paper when possible. The text paper of this book is composed in part of post-consumer waste.

Cover design: Tobias' Outwear for Books
Cover photo: © Linda Navarro

13 14 15 16 17 18 19   7 6 5 4 3 2 1

To Joshua Carter, Jordan Mae,
and Jenna Lynn who,
as children of a warrior,
have faithfully served and sacrificed
for this country since your birth.

—Marshéle Carter Waddell

To Kathleen Anne Orr
for her courage, prayers, perseverance,
and willingness to teach her warrior husband
over the past forty-four years
the artistry of loving.

—Kelly K. Orr, PhD

Contents

Contents

Acknowledgments

First, I want to thank my husband, Mark, and our three adult children, Joshua, Jordan, and Jenna, for their willingness to let me publicly share personal glimpses of our family's journey through combat-related PTSD and TBI. I salute your courage, humility, and transparency, without which this book would not exist.

Thank you to my agent, Bill Jensen, who believed in this book concept, represented it with professionalism, and found a home for it at Revell Books. Thank you to our editor, Andrea Doering, for recognizing the enormous need for this resource and for skillfully refining a rough manuscript into a polished gem. Thank you to the entire team at Baker Publishing Group for trusting us with this project.

Thank you to my coauthor and friend, Kelly Orr, PhD, for his willingness and patience to invest his military and professional experience and clinical perspective into this project. Your partnership and input transformed testimonies into tools for recovery and hope.

Thank you to my twenty-five brave sisters on the home front who contributed to the research needed for this book by participating in ten difficult interviews in eight months. Your fearless honesty will give a long-awaited voice to millions of other women who are passing through someplace dark and will remind them that they are not alone. I love each one of you.

I owe new kneepads to all of our prayer warriors. Thank you to my mother, Joyce Carter, Nancy Crabtree, James Scott, Julia Warton, DiAnna Steele, Judy Dunagan, Mark Bubeck, Kelly and Kathy Orr, Mari Pena, Nina Deeds, Doris and Stan Mincks, Suzanne Baldwin, Larry and Cassie Shafer, Bob and Kathleen Dees, Jack Aylesworth, Elaine Sellner, Rayetta Nathe, Victor and Susan Medina, Mechelle and Richard Thurston, Heather, Geoff and Matt Radler, Mark and Becky Walker, Mark Rader, Bob and Linda Swales, Pat Hobin, Jenny and Michael Sharpe, Penny Monetti, Jocelyn Green, Tanya Brown, Lorraine Pintus, Trudy Jerman, Lisa Holstein, and our twenty-five interviewees for approaching God's throne on our behalf and swinging your sword with accuracy.

Thank you for those who generously contributed content to this effort: Dr. Mark I. Bubeck, Patricia Smith, Judy Jordan, MD, Marilyn Lash, MSW, Shannon Wexelberg, John and Karen Blehm, Military Ministry Press, and New Hope Publishers.

Thank you to Therese and Tom Moncrief for opening your guest home in Fort Worth to me, where I wrote many of these pages and found comfort in your timely friendship. Thank you to Larry and Cassie Shafer for a writer's hideaway with hot lattes and an inspiring view of Pike's Peak. Thank you to Kathy Orr who brought me hot echinacea tea, throat lozenges, and tissues like clockwork as we raced toward deadline during a February Colorado snowstorm. And thank you to all the strangers who put up with my clumsy elbows and keyboard-tapping fingers as I wrote most of this manuscript in seat 9D on many flights to and from retreats for wounded warriors' wives across the country.

Thank you to our readers in this generation and in the ones to come. Be encouraged.

I also want to acknowledge those who opposed me every step of the way. The persecution only fueled my perseverance. God has and will continue to use the division and pain meant for harm and will transform it for our good. PS, I forgive you.

—Marshéle Carter Waddell

First, I want to thank my wife, Kathy, for her courage and perseverance in the face of multiple challenges. Your encouragement to pursue this project is but another example of your faith in my abilities that has often been stronger than my own. This book is a tribute to your belief that there are many ways for a warrior to show up to fight a battle.

I also want to thank Bill Jensen, for believing in this book concept and finding a home for it at Revell Books. Thank you, Andrea Doering, our editor, for listening to our ideas and making the manuscript into a cutting-edge resource. Thank you, Baker Publishing Group, for your trust and acceptance of this project.

Thank you to my coauthor and friend, Marshéle Carter Waddell, for her invitation and trust to partner in this project. Your transparency, candor, persistence, and energy are unparalleled. The words on these pages reflect the truth of your testimony that hope and strength are found in faith in a Faithful God.

I, too, want to thank the twenty-five amazing wounded warrior wives on the home front for their contribution to the research needed for this book. Your frank answers to difficult, and sometimes painful, questions are inspirations for countless others who share similar stories and who will gain strength and courage from your example. I am humbled by your courage.

Thank you to my Bible study group members, Kathy Orr, Rob and Sherry Sayers, Dean and Deena Mills, Danny and Irene Holt, Mike and Debbie Wermuth, Jim and Sarah Myers, Mike and Kris Davis. Thank you for being the prayer warriors you are and the unceasing intercession at God's throne as this book took shape.

To Dr. Mark I. Bubeck, Patricia Smith, Judy Jordan, MD, Marilyn Lash, MSW, Shannon Wexelberg, Military Ministry Press, and New Hope Publishers: thank you for your generosity in contributing to the content of this effort.

To the many men and women who over the years have so candidly shared their hopes and dreams, pains and disappointments, and along the way taught me the art of listening: thank you for your courage in letting me walk with you for a while.

To my children, Lori and Christian, Kristopher and Cheri, and the grandkids: Caleb, Samuel, Annalise, Ethan, Aaron, Noah, Isaiah, and Aubrey . . . Aslan's Apprentices . . . thank you for filling my days with sunshine and laughter!

To you, the reader, thank you for turning the pages of this book. Walk with us a while and be encouraged.

—Kelly K. Orr, PhD

Introduction

You will not fear . . . the pestilence that stalks
in the darkness.

Psalm 91:5–6

I hate what war did to my family. I hate what two wars did to
the man I married and what a third threatens to do to our
son. And, with the same measure of hatred, I loathe what war did
to the rest of us who love these two men.

Martin Luther wrote, "If you want to change the world, pick up
your pen and write." I accept that challenge and open my laptop
and my heart in order to change the world for those who love a
combat veteran and who live in the wake of the sword.

When my U.S. Navy SEAL husband returned from Iraq with only
a broken leg, I praised God that he was home safe and sound. In
the months that followed his homecoming, I sensed that his leg was
the least of our concerns. Although he was recovering physically,
his soul still walked with a limp. His unseen wounds caused by
war zone experiences went unmentioned and untreated. Slowly but
surely these invisible injuries infected our marriage, our children,

and our family life. He was home with us in body, but in his spirit a war still raged. From irritability and irrationality to nightmares and emotional paralysis, it became clear that my veteran husband was suffering from post-traumatic stress. For two years Mark denied any need for help and unintentionally led our family into a land of silent suffering.

For more than two decades our marriage had survived everything a special operations career could throw at us: frequent deployments, long separations for training and real world conflicts, serious injuries and surgeries, as well as multiple overseas family moves. The stress of my husband's job was nothing new for either of us. That may explain why my husband's frustrations and underlying anxieties caused me no new concerns at first. It was "all systems normal" and "steady as she goes," or so I thought. My first book and its companion Bible study were penned before I knew anything about the beast that would raise its ugly head when Mark returned from the frontlines.

I was not alone. As I prepared this book, I wanted others to share as well. Twenty-five women stepped forward and opened their lives to us. Here, and throughout the book, their thoughts and strategies will give insights—and a fellowship—as we journey toward hope and healing.

He was angry, depressed, and short fused.

He would throw himself into his work because that was where he was most comfortable and able to control his issues.

My son had nightmares and attempted suicide.

My husband would be talking and while in mid-sentence he would just stop and go blank in his eyes. After we shook him or nudged him while saying his name, he would finally return to reality and wonder what had happened.

He kept a light on and slept with a gun. He drank excessively.
He even ran around in the woods and around the house wear-
ing his BDUs, carrying his rifle at times.

I have friends more noble than I who bravely state that they are
thankful for the war. That sounds absurd except to those who know
either by faith or from experience that there is purpose in pain and
a gift only found in grief. I don't doubt their sincerity for I know
their hearts and I cherish their friendship. They can honestly say
they are thankful for how the fallout at home that followed the
fight overseas has resulted in a closer walk with God, a deeper faith
in His goodness and the ability to embrace each moment with an
attitude of gratitude.

I have read the work of subject-matter experts who gloss over
the horrors of post-traumatic stress disorder (PTSD), attempting
to soothe the sting and silence the cry of a nation's soul by saying
it's all good. They applaud the attainment of a sullen, resigned
thankfulness as evidence of a full and admirable recovery. They
even go so far as to rename it post-traumatic *growth*.

Well, it's *not* all good. There's a reason those who pass through
this dark place call it hell on earth. And before anyone quotes Romans 8:28[1] to me, let me be the first to say that I believe with all
my heart that God can transform for the greater good and for His
glory anything that the enemy means for our harm.

Still, am I thankful for the war? Frankly, I'm not there yet.
I aspire to offer the "hard *eucharisteo*" that Ann Voskamp so
beautifully illustrates in her book *One Thousand Gifts*. She states,
"The holy grail of joy is not in some exotic location or some
emotional mountain peak experience. The joy wonder could be
here! Here, in the messy, piercing ache of now, joy might be—un-
believably—possible!"[2] Giving thanks in all circumstances is very
difficult when it involves pulling the shards and slivers of shattered
dreams out of one's heart daily with no end to the confusion or
chaos in sight.

He has trust issues, has trouble showing love, compassion, and empathy, and is very forgetful. It is hard to get him motivated. He has started drinking again, which frightens me.

Our whole family worried ourselves to death. We never knew what was going to happen next. I even had a nervous breakdown and lost my job.

My grandchildren never got to know their father, my son. They had to live without him for years while he was incarcerated for firing a gun in public in the middle of a flashback.

When a person is close to a vet with PTSD, it changes her whole world in a negative way. She feels she is always walking on eggshells. Life is completely unpredictable. She loses trust in her spouse. It can be one of the hardest things a family has to suffer.

I still wake up every morning hating what war did to my family. Plain and simple. I didn't ask for this. I don't like the stigma and struggle of it one bit, but I believe I'm moving in the general direction of being able to honestly say one day that war's aftermath on the home front delivered priceless treasures of tried and true character, that it forged and fortified my dearest relationships, and refined us all to an impenetrable, polished perfection.

It is a fragile hope of personal and family wholeness I hold with the utmost care. I cup it gingerly in my palm and lift it heavenward daily, asking God to continue to give it life and breath. I see God and His love in the smallest steps of progress. Even so, combat-related PTSD on the home front remains the ugliest and longest battle we who share this address have ever known.

He had angry outbursts, was unloving and disengaged from our family. He had recurring nightmares and experienced insomnia.

He was a changed man. He was very easily startled, hyper-vigilant, quick to anger, frustrated, and thought his life was ruined. He did not look at me the same, kept his distance from us, didn't sleep well, and kept saying he was fine.

He didn't want to seek help, refused to discuss communication issues. He didn't want affection and could not show affection.

I often don't feel I can fully count on him. He has had a difficult time taking anything seriously. He often blows off things that are important, like deadlines, appointments, and other commitments.

I have tried countless times to talk with him about his symptoms, but he refuses. He immediately closes his eyes, drops his head, and puts his hands up. He doesn't want to talk about it. He shuts down and wants to be left alone. How I miss the love we once shared.

I miss being able to talk about anything and everything. Now we have a long list of topics that cannot be discussed.

PTSD is not new. After the Civil War our nation called it soldier's heart. World War I and II vets knew it as shell shock and battle fatigue. After the Korean and Vietnam wars, exasperated experts lumped all the surfacing symptoms together and labeled it the Vietnam Syndrome. Only in 1994 did the American Psychiatric Association officially name and define what is now known as post-traumatic stress disorder.[3] Currently, the Veterans Administration and the National Center for PTSD are hammering out yet another new definition, phrasing it as a "failure to recover."[4]

Some of the best contemporary descriptions I have found come from *War and the Soul: Healing Our Nation's Veterans from*

Post-traumatic Stress Disorder, by Edward Tick, PhD. "Veterans know that, having been to hell and back, they are different. We expect them to put war behind them and rejoin the ordinary flow of civilian life. But it is impossible for them to do so—and wrong of us to request it. When (a Viet Nam veteran) was asked when he left Viet Nam, he answered, 'Last night. It will be that way till my soul leaves this old body.' When the survivor cannot leave war's expectations, values, and losses behind, it becomes the eternal present. This frozen war consciousness is the condition we call post-traumatic stress disorder." And, "Though the affliction that today we call post-traumatic stress disorder has had many names over the centuries, it is always the result of the way war invades, wounds and transforms our spirit."[5]

There is much talk about a "new normal" for returning veterans and their families. We know full well that the place we used to live is no longer on the map. We've tried to find it, but the inner, nasal GPS voice repeats "recalculating" as we try to navigate the post-combat, civilian landscape.

He was angry and short-tempered. He had no tolerance for anything, drove fast, listened to dark music, and talked war.

He was here physically, but still over there mentally.

He lied continually. He was secretive, sad, and had more than one nightmare nightly. He combined sleeping pills with alcohol. He lost weight. He was angry with God.

He would leave the house many times a day with no explanation.

He has developed a habit of not being completely truthful. He has pursued emotional and physical relationships outside of our marriage.

At social events and in public, he was on the lookout, always on guard watching the crowd.

He often cries in his sleep.

Wounded Warrior, Wounded Home is written for those whose lives are connected to the life and service of a combat veteran. The home front needs the hope found in the voices of real families living victoriously in the aftermath of war and the signature wounds of the present conflicts: post-traumatic stress disorder and traumatic brain injury. We, the spouses and family members who love and live with these combat veterans, navigate a road with unfamiliar dangers no one prepared us to face. Military marriages, extended families, churches, and entire communities come under stress when they can no longer find the sense of "normal" they had before.

My husband suffered quietly and I, in my naïveté, ignored the signs for way too long. Society, the government, and the VA systematically ignored PTSD in the '60s and '70s. It left the combat vets with the unspoken message "Just get over it." When he first came home from Vietnam, he spoke freely of the country and the people, not necessarily about the battles, but as time wore on and people began to shun him, he stopped talking. Then people stopped asking and avoided the issue. Then he began to stuff it and went twenty years or more without wanting to talk about it at all.

I have the privilege of co-authoring this book with my friend and mentor, Kelly Orr, PhD, a clinical psychologist and Vietnam veteran. *Wounded Warrior, Wounded Home* is a combination of research and vetted stories about today's military spouses, parents, children, and grandparents—heroes on the home front who deal with the fallout of PTSD and TBI (traumatic brain injury). The story of my own special operations family's journey of faith through multiple combat deployments, which resulted in severe and chronic post-traumatic stress and extensive, multiple, moderate traumatic brain injuries, is the narrative thread that weaves together a book of hope and healing.

I believe the aftermath of war is a battle fought *and won* on the home front. We, the spouses, children, family, and friends of United States service members, urgently need to understand the warrior's heart and to arm ourselves with the biblical truth necessary to heal from combat-related stress at home.

When a veteran suffers from post-traumatic stress and/or traumatic brain injury, every member of his or her immediate family experiences the effects and, in many cases, suffers what is known as secondary acute stress. This secondary traumatic stress resembles the universal and potentially complicated process of grief. Spouses, parents, and children of warriors pass through phases of shock and confusion, hurt, anger, guilt, fatigue, fear, and finally, acceptance.

Even with faith, courage, and the discernment to apply God's promises to a very dark situation, the results of war can be emotionally scarred homes, major depression, addictive behavior, substance abuse, divorce, or suicide. However, with accurate biblical guidance, targeted prayer, professional Christ-honoring counseling and resources, informed community and church support, these same individuals and families can find hope, healing, and wholeness.

I believe a better PTSD is possible. At the start, PTSD is a viral "pestilence that stalks in the darkness" and as a result every member of the veteran's family experiences the "pain of the shattered dream." However, each of us reaches a fork in the road, a place where we must decide whether to stay stuck or to press forward toward the light. I have decided not to let this portion of my journey be the end of my joy. I remind myself frequently that this shadowed part of the path is not my permanent address. To me, PTSD has come to mean we are "passing through someplace dark." I believe that PTSD, plus the power of God, can become something much different: "peace in the shadow of the Divine," a place where our Wounded Healer waits with outstretched arms.

It is my prayer that *Wounded Warrior, Wounded Home* will guide you in constructing your own plan for physical, emotional, and spiritual wholeness, will honor you for your personal sacrifice and service to your nation, and will inspire you to re-engage in compassionate service in your community as a part of your own healing.

While I can't yet say I'm thankful for the war, I can say I'm thankful that I'm not alone. There are millions of us whose lives are connected to a combat veteran. To date, 1.5 million troops have fulfilled 3 million deployment billets to Iraq and Afghanistan. Most service members have served at least two and some as many as nine combat tours of duty. This operational tempo translates to exponential demands on the home front and compounded effects of war on the warrior. Between 30 and 40 percent of returning veterans today show symptoms of PTSD or report conditions of TBI.[6] TRICARE, the military health care provider, reports that troops and their family members make and keep 100 thousand appointments for mental health care daily.[7]

Since 2000, traumatic brain injury has been diagnosed in about 180,000 service members, the Pentagon says. But some advocates for patients say thousands more have suffered undiagnosed brain injuries. A RAND study in 2008 estimated the total number of service members with TBI to be about 320,000.[8]

Each service member's war experiences and injuries *directly impact at least three and as many as ten immediate family members and friends.* This means that at least 4.5 million and as many as 15 million close family members and friends are deeply impacted by combat stress, PTSD, and/or TBI from the wars in Iraq and Afghanistan alone. This figure does not include the lingering effects of war on the families of World War II, the Korean War, the Vietnam War, or the first Persian Gulf War veterans.

History tells us that you and I aren't odd, crazy, or the anomaly. In fact, post-combat deployment experiences on the home front are the rule rather than the exception. "Scholars have determined that during the 5,600 years of written history, 14,600 wars have been waged, that is two or three wars for every year."[9] This doesn't take into consideration the countless battles and wars that didn't have a decisive outcome that could be determined by the experts. The number of family members who have loved and lived with history's combat veterans is immeasurable. It would be simpler to count those who have not had direct military experience. In other words, there are more folks who understand and can relate to our challenges than folks who blink back at us with nothing to say or offer. Based on recorded history, we who have been directly or indirectly touched by war and its aftermath are not alone—not now, not ever.

He can't seem to concentrate or focus. He easily switches from one activity to another. He will rake leaves for ten minutes, then go to the garden to pull weeds, then leaves that to take on another "necessity." Even when he sits in his chair to read, something else will come to his mind and he'll jump up.

His driving is erratic. He swerves to avoid something in the road that most people would simply drive over.

He has been hospitalized for suicidal ideation and an actual attempt.

When he gets really angry, I can see fear in his eyes.

Our sons learned early on to ask, "Is this a good day or a bad day, Daddy?"

The bravest people I know are the women who agreed to share their stories with us for the purposes of this book. They are people like you, who are on a similar journey from combat stress toward individual and family wholeness. We are grateful for their courage and transparency. We also appreciate the generous input of various credentialed professionals and organizations that contributed to the accuracy of the clinical content.

I'm also thankful to know God is in control. The best news is that we serve a Savior who sympathizes with us and stands near to help us. Jesus invited the disciple who doubted to touch His hands and side. The nail prints in His hands and the scar under His heart were wounds of warfare in the ultimate battle He fought for our souls. Jesus said, "Put your finger here; see my hands. Reach out your hand and put it into my side. Stop doubting and believe."[10] His words were an invitation to believe, to trust the only one whose battle wounds can heal those of all others. Jesus extends the same invitation today to scarred warriors and their families: to reach out in faith and touch the Christ who bore in His body on the cross all the injuries we cause one another, both seen and unseen.

Jesus knows a warrior's heart and can make it whole again. He also recognizes the cry of the warrior's family. Our Warrior, who was wounded for our ultimate protection and freedom, has promised to present us perfect, complete, and spot free to our heavenly Father one day.[11]

I hate what war did and still does to my family. Yet I am committed to finding the growth, the good, and the hidden gifts that God alone can reveal over time. I invite you to travel with me on a road toward a new PTSD: Peace in the shadow of the Divine.

1

Wounded Warrior, Wounded Home

The Wound

Do you see it?
It's there, right here.
People don't get it. What do they think we do?
Do they even have a clue?
I doubt it.

Sometimes I think they're the lucky ones.
I know that's not really true but
You see theirs; people get theirs.

Here it is again.
You still can't see it?
It's the misplaced anger
The harsh look
The tense-fired reply
The unbridled rage
The rigid stance

The misunderstanding
The lack of compassion
The blind eye to . . .

It's easier for them.
They're finished with all of this.
They can look down and remember
Without pain.
My pain is endless
My pain will never be finished.

Does it get better?
Better than what?
I've endured this pain for years.
It becomes more difficult each time because
It mixes with the past
The past anger, the past hurts,
The past rejections, the past pains
It's all so complicated
The dream, where did it go?

The shrapnel pierced the helmet.
The IED pierced the armor.
The bullet pierced the head.
A family mourns.
A father is dead.

You still don't see it? Amazing.
I give up.
So fresh. So obvious.
To me.
It's the wound in my heart.

Judy S. Jordan, MD

No one sees the worry that weighs my heart down today; but it's there. The vital organ designed to pump life through my body is reduced to a sad sack of stones today. It hangs so low inside my chest that it tugs on my lungs and makes breathing no longer involuntary.

No one sees the lead in my legs either, but it's there. I am not *running* errands today; I am trudging, inching, slugging my way around town trying to check a few boxes off my to-do list, which because of my heavy heart and leaden legs has become an I-can't-put-these-things-off-any-longer-must-do list.

No one sees the grief growing in my gut or the sorrow sprawling across my soul or the panicked emotions that claw at my inner self.

We took our son to the airport yesterday. My husband, our youngest daughter, and I walked him as far as security where we had to say our goodbyes. I thought that no one would see this either. The TSA employee at the entrance to the line must have seen the tension across my brow. She must have noticed how I hugged my son differently, how I kissed his cheek repeatedly with intention, how I handed him a sealed handwritten letter and reluctantly pulled myself away. She tried to comfort me by telling me that my son would be home for Christmas break before I knew it.

My husband politely told her he was going to war, not to college. She responded with a loud "Oh, Jesus!" that only a middle-aged African American woman can belt out. She quickly followed her exclamation with an announcement, "In the name of Jesus, he will come home safely!" The dozen travelers in line around my son looked our direction. Her proclamation silenced the zipping and unzipping of carry-ons and stilled the slipping off of shoes and belts for a few surreal seconds. I could tell by their expressions and the eye contact a few of them bravely made with me that all of our varied lives, backgrounds, and travel plans were not as important as this intersection of clarity.

My son was the only one who did not look in our direction. He marched on smartly through security, put his shoes on and slipped his belt back through its loops. Then he turned toward us, lifted his opened hand in a motionless wave of goodbye and paused. He didn't tear up. He didn't smile. He lowered his hand, turned, and joined the travelers flowing through the Dallas/Fort Worth terminals.

That's when I heard it. That's when I heard the sound of the son-shaped piece of me being torn from the fabric of my heart. No one else heard the rend. No one else saw the fissure. I stood there, lost and looking for the faith to put one foot in front of the other to walk upright out of the airport.

I headed back to the car arm in arm with my daughter Jenna. We wiped away hot tears, walking beside my husband, Mark, a disabled combat veteran of the wars in the Balkans and Iraq. His face was tight. Few know the fear and feelings of a veteran father who must send his only son into a war his generation didn't finish. We drove home in an awkward silence as Fort Worth awakened to a typically quiet Sunday morning.

"You never know what's really going on in people's cars, do you." Mark's comment stirred the quiet. I wondered what was going on in my husband's head as we followed the curling cloverleaf highway that split to the left. A pickup truck with too much testosterone cut us off. We swerved. Mark laid on his horn. I closed my eyes and defaulted to the Lamaze breathing techniques I learned twenty-five years ago. I remembered how Joshua's first deployment to Afghanistan just last year had triggered my husband's post-traumatic stress disorder before, during, and after our son's eight-month stint. The nightmares and flashbacks of events from his own deployments to Operation Iraqi Freedom mixed with a father's love for his son were a dangerous combination for an entire year.

We weaved our way through a sleepy Fort Worth, taking the potholed side roads back to the house. The trek reminded me of the best definition I've heard for traumatic brain injury[1]: the "interstate" is closed and the "driver" must find detours and shortcuts to arrive at the destination.

I blinked back the realization that the coming year might be a messy rerun, not only for Mark, but for the entire circle of our family and close friends who have endured the dirty bombs of PTSD and TBI on our home front for nearly a decade.

PTSD and TBI are acronyms that weren't included in the Militarese 101 syllabus that Uncle Sam issued to new military spouses in the early '80s. Combined with his two broken legs, broken back, neck, nose, and blown-out ear drum, these two war wounds were the deciding factors that maxed out my husband's 100 percent disability rating at the time of his retirement. (When I share this list of service-related injuries and conditions, he frequently reminds me not to leave out the hemorrhoids.)

PTSD and TBI are the signature wounds of the wars in Iraq and Afghanistan. They are referred to as the invisible wounds of war. However, just because something is invisible doesn't mean it isn't there. And its existence can have a profound impact on the quality of our lives.

We depend on many things every day that our eyes cannot see: air that fills our lungs, gravity that keeps our feet, cars, and buildings anchored to the ground, and music that lifts our spirits. If we could see the electromagnetic activity that makes our smart phones smart, our heads would swim.

One might conclude that, in the case of air, gravity, and cyberspace, invisibility is a gracious act of the Creator, a loving selectivity that reduces the visual stimuli we must navigate every day. But what about the dark side of invisibility? What about the unseen dangers and dilemmas that our eyes cannot detect like salmonella, E.coli, and carbon monoxide? If we could see the microbes that float and piggyback their way into our nostrils and mouths from everyday activities, we probably would wear latex gloves and face masks 24/7 and never drive through for a burger again.

Technically, germs aren't invisible at all. More accurately, they are *inconspicuous*. Like PTSD and TBI, they are *invisible* only in that they are not readily seen by those not trained or equipped to detect them. They are *inconspicuous* because they are concealed.

Time and proximity to the traumatized survivor remove the camouflage. Eventually, these invisible wounds are "seen" by those of us who love and live with our veterans. The damage on deep, hidden levels bubbles to the surface and becomes evident.

Pain of the Shattered Dream

While he was still on active duty my husband's invisible wounds continued to whisper. After several more combat deployments, his wounds were hemorrhaging and demanding to be seen and treated. Mark was diagnosed with chronic and severe PTSD, and a few years later more tests confirmed that Mark had incurred multiple and extensive traumatic brain injuries from his combat service. In some respects, it helped to know what we were dealing with as a couple and as a family. Finding the name for a cluster of disturbing symptoms is always a relief of sorts to the one who suffers and for his closest family and friends. It gave us an initial fresh dose of hope that we could find a way to make things better. Yet the comfort of the diagnosis was bittersweet; we were still faced with shattered dreams.

In his book *Shattered Dreams*, Larry Crabb boldly states what we all have thought on occasion but kept to ourselves. "Sometimes God seems like the least responsive friend I have. . . . My real problem with God becomes apparent when long-held and deeply cherished dreams are shattered and He does nothing. And these are good dreams, not dreams of riches or fame, but dreams of decent health for those I love and for good relationships among family and friends. . . . Live long enough, and dreams important to you will shatter. Some will remain shattered. God will not glue together the pieces of every Humpty Dumpty who takes a great fall in your life."[2] Crabb spends the next nineteen chapters explaining that until we learn to see things rightly, "things" being God and the dreams He allows to shatter, we will stay stuck in a dark place faced with the greatest temptation of all, the temptation to lose hope in God.

I began to see things rightly at my first counseling appointment. Mark and I both knew that something was terribly wrong on the home front, but were not able to find the source of the problem on our own. I suggested that we go to counseling to find some answers. At the time, he was serving as the Director of Operations at Naval Special Warfare Group TWO, training, manning, and deploying and redeploying hundreds of SEALs to two war fronts between his own multiple deployments. His schedule was bursting at the seams, and he was adamant that the problem was mine, not ours, and certainly not his. I knew that if I didn't find some help soon, my own sanity and our marriage and home life would implode. I was in a dark place, faced with the greatest temptation of all, the temptation to lose hope in God. I walked into my first counseling session not sure what I would find, a bit embarrassed to have sunk so low that I needed mental health care, but desperate for any help.

I had dreaded the exhausting process of bringing a total stranger up to speed on my life. We were years deep into this mess. We had wandered so long inside this maze that I was convinced no one could ever find us. Yet somehow I knew that if I didn't allow the wounds to be reopened, irrigated, scraped, and allowed to regenerate new life that the injuries would turn gangrenous and we'd be done. I explained to my newfound "best friend" that not only had my husband changed since returning from combat, but that I, too, had changed. I told her that I was worried about myself and concerned for my own sanity. I described to her my constant confusion, my jumpiness, my short fuse, my difficulty sleeping, and my bouts with uncontrollable sobbing.

With a quivering chin, I timidly whispered, "Is PTSD contagious?"

She sighed and sent a sympathetic, knowing smile in my direction. I fully expected her to find humor in my naïve question and to reassure me that PTSD was certainly not infectious.

"Yes, you could say that PTSD is contagious." Her answer made me lightheaded. "Everyone who lives with a traumatized person is affected and can begin to speak and behave in ways that mirror his words and actions."

I swallowed hard.

"You are experiencing what's called acute stress, secondary traumatic stress, and compassion fatigue."[3]

I was a doe in the headlights. "How long have I got, Doc?"

One morning, while feeling particularly down, I curled up on the couch and just sat there thinking. I realized that I was letting my husband's mood be the pendulum for how I would feel that day. It was like I couldn't even be myself. If my husband was angry and withdrawn, I had trouble focusing on anything I needed to do that day. If I felt unloved by him, I felt like I must have done something wrong and that it was somehow my fault.

I found myself completely spacing out and not able to focus on a single task. I was so overwhelmed I couldn't think straight.

I was driving one day and swerved to miss a fast-food bag. I've always had some issues with being hypervigilant, even before I met my husband, but after being together for a while, I found myself taking on his behaviors, especially with driving.

I try to avoid being by myself.

The anxiety I felt was fed by the overwhelming feelings of helplessness, fearfulness, and preoccupation with trauma. It caused me to experience breathing difficulties, numbness, appetite changes. I lost thirty pounds in the first year. I couldn't sleep. I withdrew. I couldn't think straight or make a simple decision. I lost all self-esteem and experienced a roller coaster of anger and rage.

On my son's birthday I reminded myself all day to call him as I was working feverishly to finish my final assignment in a very difficult college course. I was so exhausted after finishing my assignment, I fell asleep. I forgot! What kind of mother doesn't call her son? I felt like the worst mother in the world. When I realize I have forgotten something, it makes me feel less of a person, messed up from the stress I did NOT ask for. I have to constantly ask myself, what am I doing? What am I supposed to be doing? God, help, please. Help me remember the little things and the big things.

I was driving down the road one day, my mind racing over a thousand different things, and I realized that I was having a difficult time breathing. I just couldn't seem to take a deep breath. I felt lightheaded.

Before our first session ended, my counselor reassured me that trauma was not terminal; however, if left untreated it could wreak havoc on our marriage, our children, our mental and physical health, and most importantly our faith.

I would have preferred that my husband join me in counseling so that together we could find answers and healing. For his own reasons, which I now respect, he was not ready. So I flew solo and continued weekly counseling for two years. Occasionally, on the days Mark knew I had been to an appointment, he would say, "So, did your counselor tell you to divorce me yet?"

The opposite was true. My counselor helped me to see our situation objectively. She assured me that I was not losing my mind. She gave me the tools I needed to interact at home in healthy, life-giving ways. She prayed with me, asking God to give me the courage to put the biblical counsel into practice.

I didn't want to just put a bandage on the problem. Given the choice between merely minimizing the impact of PTSD on our family versus trusting God in agreement with other believers for protection of our hearts and home, I chose the miraculous over the minimal.

The guidance and information I gleaned from several years of individual counseling formed a foundation on which I could more confidently stand. From this foundation, I opened my heart and extended my hands and began sharing our story. A sisterhood around the world was awakened as one by one, women whose lives are connected to a combat veteran began to respond.

One of the most difficult aspects of walking through some-place dark has been my feelings of being isolated and alone. I almost feel crippled in some ways because it has been very difficult to reach out for help and counsel. I am afraid others will judge us if and when I share. There have even been times when my husband or I have shared with others intimate details of some of our struggles and no one seemed to want to walk with us on our journey. We feel rejected in a way.

Running Toward Running Away

After multiple combat deployments to the Balkans in the late '90s and to Iraq from 2003 to 2006, my husband announced he was done. He made the decision in February to retire and by April we were civilians for the first time in more than twenty years. He didn't have to say it, but I knew from several years of observing him that he was trying desperately to leave behind the military, the wars, and their unrelenting pain for him and for our family. The nightmares, night sweats, and insomnia were the first clues. Then one margarita became two or three. Fits of rage and disproportionate anger triggered by a household with three teens were red flags. Disturbing reactions to certain sights and smells that derailed long-awaited family outings and vacations sounded alarms on the home front. His words and actions contradicted the love I knew he had for us. I knew that his behavior sprang from the indescribable memories that threatened to take his mind and spirit captive.

His were not the words and actions of the man I had married twenty-two years earlier. A certain darkness had crept over him, over our family, over the sweetness and safety of our home, all of which we had dedicated to the Lord with all of our hearts at the outset. That shadow was heavy with the stench and palpable darkness of war and its aftermath.

He couldn't drive fast enough. He couldn't get Virginia Beach and, more specifically, Naval Special Warfare out of his rearview mirror soon enough. In July our family of five left the white sands of Virginia Beach and rocketed across West Virginia, the southernmost tips of Indiana and Illinois, and into Kansas. Our rising high school senior sweat through the fever spikes of mononucleosis in the backseat and our Sheltie, the only eager one in the vehicle, panted with bad breath at my side. In strained silence, we traveled through the Appalachians, slipped through the arches at sunset in St. Louis, and killed swarms of yellow grasshoppers with our windshield for what seemed an eternity through the cornfields of Kansas. The accumulated anxieties of several years hounded us all the way to the border of Colorado.

We stopped at the Colorado state border. A pathetic, rickety sign with faded letters announced: Welcome to Colorful Colorado. Drained and pale from traveling mach speed in the dead of summer, the kids and I looked at one another. *Colorful?* The sky was milky, overcast, gray. The fields were covered in dead brown knee-high grass. There wasn't a green tree in sight. *Colorful?*

The state's welcome sign mocked and stung my heart. It added insult to injury. Our hearts longed for light, ached for vivid colors, for any signs of life outwardly and inwardly. After taking a few awkward pictures, we piled back into the Suburban. My husband floored it across the eastern plains of Colorado toward our new home, Colorado Springs.

Flat, flat, flat. Where were the grand Rocky Mountains? Where were the rolling foothills with waving wildflowers to welcome us like the ones in our Colorado calendar? I was getting worried that perhaps Mark had taken a wrong turn in his hurry to leave a quarter-century of service and sacrifice behind him.

For hours, I watched for mountain peaks to erupt on the western horizon. I imagined Colorado Springs would be flowing with . . . well, springs. Surely there would be springs of clear mountain water bubbling and giggling over smooth boulders through wide meadows of lush green grass, where we could dip our toes into refreshing waters surrounded by the heavenly grandeur of the Rockies.

More than this, we longed for springs of hope where we could find refreshment and renewal of strength for the journey, for springs of healing where we could wash the invisible wounds of war from our minds and spirits. Finally, as we crested the high plains of northeastern Colorado Springs, Pikes Peak and all her sisters, snow-dusted even in July, came into view. The mile-long wall of formidable, breathtaking summits punctured the earth's surface in the west. But the mountains did not offer the hoped-for refreshment. Later that day, after we had checked into our extended-stay hotel, I took my Sheltie out in the field. I let him off his leash and I sat on the hard ground. I was accompanied only by several scrawny, thirsty black-eyed Susans, bent over to the ground by the cutting wind. I pulled the hood of my sweatshirt up over my head, drew my knees to my chest, and had a stare-down with the Front Range. I looked up at her and she glared down at me.

The tears found their way from deep inside my wounded heart and spilled down my cheeks. I rested my forehead on my knees and sobbed. My dog nuzzled his way under my arm and into my embrace, sensing my need for company and comfort.

I embraced him and found the will to look again at the Front Range. How could something so treacherous, so inhospitable, be so attractive, I wondered. Likewise, could anything of beauty be found in this harsh, inhospitable environment of trauma and combat stress? I whispered a prayer to God, asking Him where He was in all of this.

Military life had not been easy even in peacetime. And yet we had learned its rhythms and had adapted to its demands for more than two decades. Even through real-world operations and several wars, our family had managed . . . until now. We were now facing new challenges that seemed insurmountable. I asked God if this was the end of the road for my marriage, for our family, for my hopes, and even for my faith.

Cold Shadows and Living Water

It was in Colorado Springs, at the referral of our new family doctor, that we finally sought counseling as a couple. Kelly Orr, PhD, a Christian psychologist and Vietnam veteran, equipped us to see the darkness of PTSD in a different light. In the safety of several sessions, we saw the first hint that perhaps, just maybe, God was up to something good in our lives. Even though it looked like the dead end for our dreams, God, through our own times in His Word and through the counsel of Christian medical professionals, let us know that He would be faithful to keep us as the apple of His eye, that He would hide us in the shadow of His wings.[4] Dr. Orr reassured me that as I prepared the way for the Lord, made straight paths for Him, that every valley would be filled in, every mountain and hill would be made low. The crooked roads would become straight, the rough ways smooth. And all mankind would see God's salvation.[5] It was in Dr. Orr's office, in the loving counsel and compassion of one who had "been there," that I got my first sip of hope from the springs of Living Water. I had found strength for the journey that still loomed ahead of us.

I finally knew that even as I passed through the valley of the shadow of death, I could do so without fear because the living God was with me no matter what. All He asked was that I trust Him daily. Three years and many "aha" moments later, I asked Dr. Orr if he would consider coauthoring a book with me to encourage and equip family members of combat veterans to see their situation and themselves rightly as he helped me to do. His hesitant yes both humbled and honored me. We have penned this book in tandem, believing God wants military families to know that what looks like the end of the road is really an opportunity for Him to work, for the invisible God to be revealed, and for His enemies to be crushed under the feet of our faith in Him.

God's tender love and nearness expressed through His people and His Word have changed the way I view PTSD and its effect on families. He continues to correct the way I see war's aftermath on the home front. I saw things more clearly on a recent trip to Washington, DC. While there, we decided to visit the Vietnam Veterans Memorial, known as The Wall, before sunset.

The designer of The Wall, Maya Ying Lin, purposely chose black granite for the memorial's stone mirrorlike surface when it is polished. It reflects the images of the surrounding shade trees, grassy hills, and proud monuments. What she may or may not have intended is how it changed the way I see things. As I strolled with my daughter past panel after panel filled with individual sacrifices, I saw myself. A mirror image of myself stared back at me from behind the engraved names. My reflection was superimposed over and behind and between hundreds of names. As I strolled, my life touched theirs and theirs mine from one end of The Wall to the other. Their service and their sacrifice were not solo. Nor did their lives and loss touch only the men with whom they fought. Their lives were part of my reflection and therefore part of me. My daughter and I stood there, the spouse and daughter of a combat veteran, reflected by, swallowed by, and sent by The Wall, to give voice to the countless casualties of war that still live.

Questions for Reflection

1. Have you noticed any changes in your service member's behavior or personality or habits since his/her return from war? If so, what changes have you noticed?

2. Describe one or two incidents or scenarios that *first* alerted you to changes in your service member.

3. Do you feel comfortable talking openly with your service member about his/her symptoms or struggles? If not, why?

4. Has he/she sought professional medical help or counseling services for PTSD concerns? If not, why not?

5. Would you describe your service member's symptoms as mild, moderate, or severe?

6. In your opinion, is your service member's condition improving since his/her return? If not, please explain.

7. In your own words, how does a vet's post-traumatic stress symptoms affect his/her spouse, children, and extended family members?

8. What has been the most difficult aspect of this challenge for you (feeling isolated and alone, lack of reliable information or resources, anger, sadness, fear, feeling unsafe, domestic violence, self-medicating or substance abuse, addictive behavior, helplessness, etc.)?

2

Living Grief

The Pain of the Shattered Dream

The Pain

What do you do with the pain?
What do you do with the grief?
Where do you put it?
On a shelf, high up, out of reach
Or face to face, in front of you, swallowing you
Or on a schedule, an agenda, I'll think about it later
Will there be a later for me; there wasn't for them.
Put it away; the pain's too deep, too vast, too
    unfathomable,
Too heavy, too crushing, too unbearable,
Too impossible to deal with
Put it where it's safe, where it can't touch me
Hide it,
from me,
from them,
then it goes away

Out of sight, out of mind, right?
It begins to smolder, to burn, to be transformed
Do I recognize it?
Will I recognize it?
I must cry for them; only then can I cry for me.

                                                    Judy S. Jordan, MD

Summer of Sparrows

I was in Phoenix for my annual May visit with my mother and older daughter. The afternoon Sonoran Desert sun formed new freckles on my shoulders as I waited. My mother and younger daughter, Jenna, had gone ahead into the Arizona Science Museum while I waited for my older daughter, Jordan, to park and join us to see Body Worlds. Inside, an air-conditioned exhibit of skinned cadavers, frozen midstride by formaldehyde, awaited us, along with an assortment of dyed and diseased body parts displayed in department store jewelry cases. It was May 2011, and our family was in turmoil again.

A call from my husband rattled my phone and my nerves. Our connection was bad. A dead zone of several varieties made conversation difficult. He sounded distant, distracted, frustrated. The past decade had stretched our marriage past the point of resilience and maybe return. The desert sun suddenly seemed unbearable. I stepped into the shade by the museum entrance for relief.

"Do you want to end well with me or not?"

At the same time that his question collided with my heart, a sparrow crashed into the glass front of the museum a few feet from me. She tumbled and fell lifeless, along with my heart, onto the hot sidewalk. She hadn't expected that window. I hadn't expected his words.

The loud thud of beak and wings against bulletproof glass jolted me. As I watched the sparrow's drama unfold, my husband must have thought that the pause between his question and my reply spoke for itself. She rolled over exposing her striped throat and soft brown underbelly. Her beak fell open and she panted. She closed her black eyes and exhaled, long and labored, what seemed her final breath. I couldn't catch mine.

She was I and I was she. Just seconds ago she had soared confidently, wings wide and strong and eyes clear, into her sunny day. Just the week before, Mark and I had celebrated our twenty-seventh anniversary. Wasn't it only yesterday that I, too, soared confidently on the wings of sweet new love into the challenges of married military life? She-sparrow and I had both suddenly slammed into something unplanned and impenetrable. She lay in shock on the shaded museum sidewalk. How could she have known that the lifelike images of paloverde and palm trees and open sky ahead of her were unreliable reflections of what lay behind her? She didn't see it coming. My heart and marriage lay stunned beside her, breathing what felt like their final breath, on the dark path of PTSD.

The cell dead zone resulted in a dropped call before I could answer my husband's question. My daughter arrived and we went into the museum. We strolled silently through corridors of naked corpses positioned in lifelike postures. Several cadavers stood together as in conversation, heads tilted, mouths and hands "talking." My heart ached.

I was looking at a still frame of what our family had become. We who had once breathed and believed were now dead and on display. We were going through the motions, but the lifeblood of unconditional love and godly faith that had pulsed through our family for more than two decades of demanding military life had been replaced with a putrid preservative called PTSD.

I realized again how the impact of our warrior's unresolved pain had left our entire family smelling of death. I was surrounded by dead birds, dead people, and dead dreams.

But why was I grieving? What right or reason did we who welcomed him home have to grieve? Every time I read the names in the newspaper of those killed in action or watched their names scroll silently at the end of the evening television news, I thanked God that my warrior had made it home alive after each combat deployment. And yet his changing personality and surprising words and actions made me feel otherwise.

When the PTSD symptoms first appeared I was confused. I was never sure what would happen next. Just one trigger and the whole day or evening would disintegrate. Home life was highly flammable. I didn't know whom I could trust to share my breaking heart. Seeking and finding help without dishonoring or upsetting him was a challenge. I couldn't decide how to approach the topic with him.

Then I got angry. My anger was a two-headed monster. I was angry at my warrior for his lack of self-control, for hurting my feelings, for emotionally scarring the children, for embarrassing me in front of others, for denying the existence of a problem, and for his refusal to get help.

At times I wrestled with guilt. I reasoned that if I were a better wife, a better mother, I would be handling this crisis with more grace, forgiveness, and tenderness. On my better days, I believed that by assuming all responsibilities for the family and the house I would help him heal more quickly.

Frankly, I got sick and tired of it and wanted to walk out. Part of me wanted to quit, to leave, to stop helping him, to stop loving him, to stop praying for him. The D-word crossed my mind a few times, something we promised more than two decades earlier at the altar would never be an option.

At times I had wanted to scream and demand that he leave the military, believing that by putting this way of life behind us the pain would disappear eventually. I resented having to worry that something might trigger painful memories for him. I was tempted to nag, to complain and make ultimatums. I got tired of trying, tired of listening, tired of trying to understand. I felt deep sorrow for us as a couple and as a family, for our children and for myself.

Untangling the Grief Knot

As Mark deployed repeatedly to Iraq for several years, my first counselor in Virginia Beach reassured me that I wasn't going crazy and gave
me the tools I needed to interact at home in healthy, life-giving ways.
After my husband's retirement from active duty, my next counselor,
Dr. Kelly Orr, helped me to better understand that the confusion,
anger, and guilt that our children and I were still experiencing *years
later* were all steps in the process of grief. He emphasized that the
effect invisible wounds have on family members is primarily a sense
of great loss. I asked him the question that had kept me tied in knots.

"Why am I grieving? He came home alive! What died?"

He smiled and applauded what seemed like a silly question.
He encouraged me to start my own healing process by answering
that question. He challenged me to name my losses. After exploring them for several weeks, I felt discouraged, even dizzy from the
discoveries. I told him I was tired of the emotional roller coaster.

He empathized and then enlightened me with an illustration
that has stayed with me. He said that we were experiencing a *living
grief*, the incremental dying that happens daily when individuals,
relationships, and families are severely traumatized. The healing
process requires permission to grieve that which was lost, a long-term
perspective, and a teachable heart that yearns to better understand
how we humans handle change and loss. He explained that this does
not take place on a straight, tidy timeline. He said if we could sketch
an illustration of living grief it would look more like a Celtic knot
or border design. The experience has a lot of back-and-forth movement, unexpected ups and downs, sharp turns and somersaulting
over onto itself. We are the only creatures in the universe that do not
accept the natural order of things. We are upset by change, yet those
who embrace the change and grow face the challenge of living grief.

Dr. Orr encouraged me to allow myself to mourn those things
that would never be the same again because of the war. He promised
that in time I would be able to look back over my shoulder and see

an intricate pattern made of complicated knots, hard angles, and contrasting colors, and the pattern would form a beautiful frame for God's purpose and calling on my life.

Precisely Misunderstood

The driver of the rental car courtesy shuttle welcomed me to San Diego and asked if I was there for business or pleasure. I let him know I was there on business, but that I had lived in Coronado two decades earlier when my husband was serving at SEAL Team ONE. I'm not sure where our wires got crossed, but somehow the driver understood that I *used to be* married to a Navy SEAL and now I was a war widow revisiting memories of our early marriage. Normally, I would have spoken right up to clear up the misunderstanding. Caught off guard and confused by his emotional response, my curiosity kept me quiet. I wanted to know where the conversation might go. When we arrived at the rental car lot, he leaped to lend a hand with my luggage. With sincere sympathy, he thanked me for our sacrifices and wished me a meaningful stay in San Diego. In a way I felt a bit irreverent for being the wrong recipient of KIA condolences. In another way, I was glad I had stayed quiet. His compassion and condolences spoke to a place deep within that grieved silently.

Thinking Mark would find humor in this story, I shared it with him later on the phone. He didn't laugh. Instead, he paused and then responded,

"Maybe God is trying to reveal something to you. Maybe you are a war widow on some spiritual level."

Over the next several days, when I wasn't working, I stared at the ocean, contemplating the idea that I could be a different kind of war widow.

I had also lost a loved one because of pain—pain forced on us by war and inflicted on one another by wrong choices in its aftermath.

I know cognitively that I'm not an actual gold star wife. But in a very real stabbing sense, I and millions like me are experiencing a difficult grief, one that goes on and on and on. I realized that I was exhausted, astonished at how my body was letting down and telling me it needed to slow down, to stop, to power down, to think, to stop striving, planning, fretting, denying, and running. Yet when I slowed down, I felt like crying. If I slowed down long enough, an unbearable sadness surfaced. It hurt and I didn't want to allow the sadness one inch. So I didn't slow down.

When I asked women across the country in conversation and email to name the losses that they, the loved ones of warriors with invisible wounds, experience on the home front, I found I wasn't alone in my grief.

I lost a deep sense of security in our marriage and in our future. I wonder if we will retire together and grow old together. Each time my soldier slides backward, it feels like a small tremor that could lead to another 9.9 earthquake.

I miss the nights of cuddling up and just watching movies, the sense of loving and being loved. I miss the simple things, like I-love-you kisses on the forehead. War took that from me. I really wish I knew how to get it back.

I lost the part of my husband that I should have had from the beginning but never did. I never was let into the innermost part of him, the secrets he kept, the intimate details of his life. . . . After we got married, I lost the person I had fallen in love with. Every time I get him back, he leaves me again in the worst sense possible—emotionally.

Back and forth . . .

Between the third and fourth tours to Iraq, there was a distinct change in his eyes when he looked at me. The love I used to see and feel was no longer there. It has been replaced by a look of anger, frustration, and impatience.

His desire for intimacy has changed. I have never felt less important, less loved, or less needed by my own husband. He is not tender or loving, but distant.

At times it overwhelms me and I just cry. I don't know what God has planned for us. I feel lost and wonder how are we to get through all this. I don't know what my warrior is waiting for, I have suggested counseling on several occasions, and he refuses. It continuously hurts me so deeply; this is not the man I once knew. I miss his affection so badly.

He has lost all desire for intimacy. I thought it was the different medications, the PTSD, the pain, the nightmares. As time went by, I would make advances on occasion. I was rejected time after time until I could no longer handle it. It broke my heart not being able to understand why he was pushing me away when I thought we should be running to each other for love and support.

Ups and downs . . .

I long for the marriage we used to have, the love and intimacy we once shared. This has been by far the most painful loss. I impatiently wait day after day wondering how long it will be before he is ready to re-establish "us."

My sense of security and closeness with my husband no longer exists. My security has been rocked.

We have lost time in sharing life. Due to his PTSD and other health-related issues, we cannot plan to attend any event. We can no longer travel because we need to stay near a hospital. We love the outdoors—fishing, camping, photography—but these activities are no longer possible. We haven't left our hometown in eight years.

Sharp turns and somersaults . . .

I lost my job and haven't been employed for thirteen months. Caregiving and the ongoing battle to get his much needed benefits and pay have been stressful.

Our intimacy has suffered. We lack communication.

The one thing I lost that I treasured the most is trust. I had an immense amount of trust in my husband in all areas of our lives. That trust has been shattered.

I have lost me. I used to be an outgoing, friendly person. I have become isolated. I am tired. I've also lost some friendships. There are some that will still invite us to activities. I feel very lonely at times.

Trust. Security . . .
Physical intimacy . . .
Emotional closeness . . .
Connection . . .
Communication . . .
Time . . .
Career . . .
Personal goals . . .
Creativity . . .
Friendships . . .
The me I used to be . . .
Myself.

Dr. Orr warned me to fasten my seatbelt because those in the grief process constantly move. The professionals have labeled and defined those phases in different ways.

According to author Elisabeth Kubler-Ross, MD, grief is a five-stage process: denial, anger, bargaining, sadness, and finally acceptance.[1] Denial is the first step toward acceptance. In this phase we see compulsive choices and addictive behaviors in ourselves. We don't want to face the facts. Anger, the next necessary step toward acceptance, boils down to blaming others, blaming God, blaming self. Bargaining is the season in which we try to make a deal with the circumstances. We try to negotiate with reality. If I do A, then B will happen. Then, finally, deep sorrow sets in. We cry the stinging tears of surrender and make room for the change that has happened. Throughout the process, acceptance is the goal.

Nurse practitioner Elizabeth Sikes offers another sequence: numbness, denial, despair, detachment, and recovery.[2] Numbness is associated with shock. We go about life mechanically, able only to go through the motions. During denial, we experience disbelief, anger, low self-esteem. We cry, feel weak and nauseated. We lose our appetites and aren't able to sleep well. Numbness and denial give way to despair. We feel we are going crazy. We plummet into depression. We are slow in thought and in action. We try to recover the one we "lost" by taking on that person's personality traits. Finally we arrive at a bridge to the new normal, which Sikes calls detachment. We withdraw from normal activities and isolate ourselves from the world. We feel disorganized and apathetic. We have zero spontaneity and display a bland facial expression. Finally, we experience recovery. Our loss hurts less. We are able to remember more comfortably and more realistically both the good and the bad of our yesterdays.

Loss happens. It's a sad but inevitable piece of life. We lose people through death, divorce, geographic moves, and alienation. We also lose things in our own lives such as careers, health, and opportunities. The challenge is to learn to deal with each loss in such a way as to promote growth and faith.

Loss is a dark and strange place to navigate alone. As we encounter the stages of grief brought on by PTSD and TBI, support groups and counseling environments provide safe havens for us.

Jesus has firsthand experience with invisible wounds. The prophet Isaiah described Jesus as despised, forsaken of men, a man of sorrows, and acquainted with grief.[3] According to the writer of the book of Hebrews, Jesus "was in all points tempted as we are, yet without sin." And because He empathizes with our weaknesses, we can "come boldly to the throne of grace, that we may obtain mercy, and find grace to help in time of need."[4] We who wrestle with the invisible wounds of war on the home front have an Advocate in heaven who's been there.

At the start of Jesus' earthly ministry, He announced that He was the fulfillment of the prophecy of Isaiah 61:1–3.

> The Spirit of the Sovereign LORD is on me, because the LORD has anointed me to proclaim good news to the poor. He has sent me to bind up the brokenhearted, to proclaim freedom for the captives and release from darkness for the prisoners, to proclaim the year of the LORD's favor and the day of vengeance of our God, to comfort all who mourn, and provide for those who grieve in Zion—to bestow on them a crown of beauty instead of ashes, the oil of joy instead of mourning, and a garment of praise instead of a spirit of despair. They will be called oaks of righteousness, a planting of the LORD for the display of his splendor.[5]

Jesus was describing the spectrum and the continuum of the grieving process, the way a person of faith moves through mourning toward healing and into becoming an example of hope to others not too far behind him or her. He was boldly declaring that He was sent to walk with us every step of the way through every season of loss and recovery.

In the book *How People Grow*, authors Henry Cloud and John Townsend say that grief is different from all other pain for two reasons. First, it is "a process we enter into somewhat voluntarily." We experience losses and pain as no choice of our own. But to let go and deal with them, we have to turn our face toward the grief process. That is probably one reason why the Bible encourages us to grieve, as an act of wisdom. Solomon says,

> It is better to go to a house of mourning than to go to a house of feasting. . . . Sorrow is better than laughter, because a sad face is good for the heart. The heart of the wise is in the house of mourning, but the heart of fools is in the house of pleasure. [6]

The second reason is that grief "is the pain that can heal all other pains. It is the most important pain." When we grieve, we let go of something. We get past it. We send it away. We move on. Then whatever the *it* was can be over.[7] In Christ, there is a gift found only in grief, a love realized only through loss. "Though he brings grief, he will show compassion, so great is his unfailing love."[8]

His Eye Is on the Sparrow

When we exited the museum, I couldn't help but look for the fallen sparrow. She was there, but, to my surprise, she was on her feet. She steadied herself on the shaded sidewalk, catching her breath and blinking her eyes. She shivered once or twice, shaking off the last of the sudden impact, then flitted away to safety under a boxwood hedge. She began to rummage in the brown mulch for a sprig of grass, a seed, a twig—supplies for her home-improvement project. She returned to the task at hand. She returned to building and repairing her house.

Beginning in chapter three, we will fly at a lower altitude through chapter six to provide more context and color for each part of the living grief journey that we who care for a combat veteran are on. Our prayer is that your understanding will deepen, that you will see yourself reflected in the unfolding testimonies and anecdotes, and that you will give yourself the freedom to fully grieve your losses that have resulted from the changes you've bravely faced.

Questions for Reflection

1. We have all suffered loss in our lives, but living with a traumatized individual brings with it a sense of sadness that can be overwhelming. Give some thought to what you feel has been lost as a result of your loved one's PTSD and TBI. What did you treasure that you feel no longer exists?

2. Grief refuses to be ignored. How have you seen grief bubble to the surface in your own life (e.g., increased fears, anger, depression, crying, wrestling with guilt, feeling lonely, blaming God and others, numbing, self-medicating)?

3. What have you done to move through the weight of grief in healthy ways? How do you know it's working?

4. What Scripture verses or promises have brought you the most comfort during these times?

3

Dealing with Delays, Detours, and Denied Entry

Get rid of all bitterness, rage and anger, brawling
and slander, along with every form of malice.

Ephesians 4:31

I wondered if it was spam or a scam or both. My cursor hovered over the highlighted message. Curiosity resulted in a click that opened the email with the subject line: "Will you represent our spring line?" I read and reread the unexpected message that invited me to participate in a photo shoot for the spring line of a Canadian jeans company.

An invitation to be a model? At my age? I laughed to myself and told my inner child, now bouncing up and down and begging to go, to sit down and be still. When she looked away, I looked for the delete tab. Then the teenage girl who had dreamed of becoming a high-dollar runway model, the one who had taken the expensive, cheesy modeling courses and entered (and lost) Miss Teen Arizona contests, the one I had tucked far beneath three decades of college, child rearing, and a husband's military career, tapped me on the shoulder to remind me she was still there.

The sender explained that the marketing team had read about our family online. They found our story inspiring and wanted to honor American and Canadian military families by inviting a military spouse to model their jeans. Convinced this silliness was a waste of my time, I got up to reheat my tea. When I saw myself in the microwave oven's reflection, I straightened my spine, sucked in my gut, and pooched out my rear end. My "mom jeans" ignored me and insisted on sagging in all the wrong places. Deflated, I returned to my computer, sent that email to the trash bin and continued working.

Over the next few weeks, I snooped around online just to confirm that this wasn't a joke. When four pairs of new great-fitting jeans arrived by FedEx, I was convinced it was legit and took the leap. The trip to Montreal only would take three days, I reasoned, two for travel and one for the photo shoot. I would be home in time to hang lights before the kids came home for Christmas.

We deplaned in Montreal and the first immigration officer peered at me over her unattractive rims and asked what was the nature of my visit to Montreal. I restrained myself, trying not to sound like a blond bimbo, and proceeded to tell her the truth.

"Bonjour!" I started, and with as much professionalism as I could muster in that moment, I eagerly told her that I would be a model in a photo shoot for one day and then would return to the United States. She wasn't convinced.

She handed my passport back to me and told me to wait in the immigration office behind her. I did. For the next five hours, three other immigration officers, nameless with only numbers on their chests, handcuffs and billy clubs attached to their waists, asked for papers, papers, and more papers and repeatedly interrogated me with the same three questions. My mobile phone rang and rang. The limo driver outside at the curb wanted to know where I was.

The marketing director and even the CEO of the jeans company called the customs office and tried to explain who I was and why I was there. Jacque, Pierre, and François didn't care. The jeans company apparently had not done their job properly in bringing an American citizen into Canada. They had overlooked filing one paper, an LMO, Labor Market Opinion.

I got to my hotel room at 2:00 a.m. and finally called my husband. He asked how I was. I told him that I was being deported from Canada. He laughed, yawned, and said, "No, really, nobody gets deported from Canada. How are you?" I dozed for two hours and returned, as instructed, to the immigration office before dawn. Ninety minutes later, another black-uniformed, nameless, numbered immigration officer with black steel-toed boots, billy club, and handcuffs appeared and told me to follow him. I had to trot to keep pace with his strides, all the while lugging the baggage he hadn't offered to help carry.

We stopped at a ticketing desk and waited for the first morning shift of clerks to arrive. Then he whisked me through the first of ten checkpoints: Canada TSA, Canada customs, U.S. customs, security checks, all the way to Gate 81. We drew too much attention, he in his black, fitted uniform and spit-shined work boots and I in my big over-sprayed hair, red holiday sweater, and red cowboy boots. People whispered as we walked briskly and with purpose to the head of every line, wondering if I was a visiting dignitary or even a rising rock star. I made the most of the moment, smiling and chatting with everyone en route. At every turn, my escort rudely reminded me that I was in trouble and that I had better toe the line if I ever wanted to come back to Canada. Finally at my gate, where I had touched up my make-up and practiced my *français* twelve hours earlier, he explained as if he was reading me my rights what had just happened at the last ten checkpoints. He assured me that my file wouldn't be flagged "in a bad way" should I ever attempt to return to Canada one day. *Whew,* I thought. *Not.*

I had come to Canada to donate my time, to raise awareness about the sacrifices of military families, to get the word out about post-traumatic stress and traumatic brain injuries. I had come willingly to do charitable, worthwhile work in an allied nation, our neighbors to the north, whose sons and daughters fight alongside my husband and son on the front lines of Iraq and Afghanistan. My motives were good, yet they had shut me out, keeping me in the dark as they decided what to do with me. I had been treated as suspicious and promptly sent away. I felt unwanted, unwelcome. The dream had dissolved into major disappointment.

Not in the Club

There is a lot more to this story, much of which I processed on my way home. The twenty-four hours of missing paperwork, closed borders, and locked doors left me frustrated, confused, and angry. But the closed border is the image that reminds me that in the aftermath of combat, we who love and live with a veteran encounter closed borders of communication daily. We are denied entry to those places of emotional and spiritual intimacy we once shared with our loved one. We try every tactic we know to get into the foreign land where our warrior now lives, only to realize that we are not citizens of that country.

A comment my husband made recently summed it up. The content of the sparse email messages to me from our son, who was serving in Afghanistan, was always brief and benign. However, his notes to his father, a veteran of the same war on terrorism, were more frequent and provided much more insight into our son's heart and mind. I couldn't understand why our son, with whom I had a close relationship until his first deployment, freely shared his frustrations and fears with his father and not with me. "Face it, Marshéle. You're simply not in the club," he said.

I heard the door slam and the deadbolt turn. I didn't have the correct paperwork and would not be allowed entry. Ever. No matter how I tugged and pushed, I would never be allowed in this part of his life in the same way another vet would.

Dr. Edward Tick, author of *War and the Soul*, describes the club as "the bond that develops between people under fire together. The lives of those who share the mud and danger and blood of warfare become intermingled. The power of this bond transcends all others, even the marriage and family bonds we forge in civilian life. . . . Brothers-in-arms or sisters-in-arms become like two souls having one identity."[1]

We, the family members and close friends of the warrior, push and pull against this unseen, unspoken bond. The result topples homes and breaks hearts. Yet healing can begin and closeness can be reestablished when we recognize the reason for the warrior's emotional border control.

There is a look in the eyes of a combat veteran that can only be understood by other combat veterans, according to John L. Blehm, coauthor of *Angel of Death*. Combat veterans "share a special brotherhood, forged out of the fires of hell that enables them to look at one another and think the words: 'I know.' Family members and friends do not understand my reasons for my distance and I see the bewilderment and pain in their eyes. I am afraid that I will lose them if I do not talk about this, but I am also afraid that I might lose MYSELF if I do."[2]

His Rage, My Response

Until we recognize and can respect the warrior's shift of loyalties, we family members will continue to do all the wrong things for all the right reasons. Our anger, which stems from confusion and hurt, is very real. When we admit and accept it, we can diffuse it. The day we fly full force into what appeared to be an open door, only to collide with the reality that we are not in the club, is the day we need to reassess who we are and who our loved one is *now*. Our warrior's anger is used to avoid the intrusive thoughts and emotions that come with intimacy and vulnerability. The warrior's thinking goes like this: *If I stay angry, I don't have to deal with those unwanted feelings.* The warrior is angry because of the loss of friends and the uncertainty of having lived in a totally random, unpredictable environment. The warrior is angry due to feelings of betrayal on the battlefield or of lack of empowerment to do an assigned mission. Anger, more than any other emotion, reinforces itself, because adrenaline and a sense of power accompany it. Anger can be energizing to the warrior up to a point. Veterans struggling with PTSD can perceive family members as safe targets. And, if episodic anger is allowed to continue, it becomes chronic and contemptuous.

In many ways, a warrior's anger stems from a need to control the environment. When a warrior senses he is walking into unknown territory, the emotion flares. It may have nothing to do with the context we see, and everything to do with the warrior's inner compass and context. A warrior's inner turmoil can be overwhelming for him or her. The veteran resorts to the only resource available—anger.

He expresses his anger through alcohol abuse, isolating himself from our kids and me, yelling, and physically pinning or blocking us.

He drives dangerously whether we are in the car with him or not. He overreacts and is verbally abusive at home. He threatens us with weapons.

I asked him a question about something trivial, like the carpool. I missed what he said, so I asked him again. He pushed me against the wall and yelled in my face, "You don't listen!" I took my son. We left the house for a few days and did not contact him. Later, after we returned home, he said he had nothing to apologize for, that it was his house and he would kick in the door if he wanted.

What? Me, Angry?

Mark and I have had the honor of sharing our story in many interviews for articles, radio, and television news stories. We are motivated by our conviction that our transparency and willingness will not only increase our nation's awareness of the needs on the home front, but that our story will encourage other skeptical veterans and family members to seek the necessary help without hesitation or shame.

In the early days, when I would hear Mark talking openly with reporters about our family's journey and how Hope for the Home Front began, he would look them straight in the eyes and answer, "Bottom line, my wife got angry."

Any time he said this their pencils paused and the room fell quiet. Uncomfortable with the silence that followed, someone would nervously laugh, reposition himself in the chair, and the interview would continue. Mark never batted an eye. He meant it.

The first few times I heard him say this, I pursed my lips and thought loudly, *What? Me, angry? You're off base, Honey. I'm not angry at all! I'm the peacemaker in this home.* I told myself that my being perturbed was only his perspective brought on by his PTSD. So each time I would smile sweetly and shrug my shoulders at the reporters. And yet he continued to say this in interviews across the nation.

It started to irritate me. I felt his comment misrepresented me. I didn't want to be portrayed as the angry wife. I was brought up to be a genteel lady of the Southern variety. A disgruntled, abrasive woman did not fit that image. I was convinced that love alone had propelled my incessant drive to learn about post-traumatic stress and traumatic brain injury and to communicate that to a country on the cusp of helping millions of veterans and family members heal from combat.

Over the years, his "my-wife-got-angry" comment echoed in my ears and began to dovetail with others' take on the matter. A handful of close friends, all on separate occasions, asked me pointed questions and made gentle, yet inescapable, references to the curtness and fatigue in my voice, the tension that kept my forehead tight and my fuse short. My mother pointed out to me that my smile wasn't genuine any longer. She said my face was strained, that my eyes were dark and blank, cradled by dark circles. She said my mouth smiled, but my eyes didn't anymore.

My first response to her was, *Oh, I'm just tired.* Like Mark had done earlier, she didn't bat an eye. Reluctantly, I followed the breadcrumbs farther back on the PTSD trail and slowly began to see that anger was indeed the source of my bullheaded bulldozing and exhaustion. The unacknowledged anger had sucked the smile right out of my eyes, and bitterness had infused my words with a hard edge. My repressed rage against the effects of war that had come home with my warrior drew bluish purple rings around my eyes.

Why Am I So Angry?

We make our anger wait or we tell ourselves it's not really anger—but we on the home front have a lot to be angry about. I was mad at myself, my circumstances, my vet for coming back so changed, mad at the military, mad at God for allowing the trauma, mad at friends who don't seem to have a clue, and mad at the dog for barking. And I was angry at the unseen entity, the invisible force that was holding my best friend, my lover, and my children's father hostage.

I felt shut out, always trying to offer help or to persuade my loved one to seek help, trying to keep peace in the home and in family relationships, trying to figure out my warrior's withdrawal, isolation, his not-open-for-business moods, and his shocking reactions to situations that were either normal or inconsequential to the rest of us.

I suppressed my anger as best as I could during this time. I saw my veteran unraveling so I felt I had no choice but to hold it together for the sake of my family. My anger came out in the form of a lot of crying in the middle of the night when no one else was awake. The repressed anger also resulted in some depression.

I felt angry when my husband lied to me or came home intoxicated because I felt betrayed, alone, and insecure. I felt my whole world could come crumbling down and my marriage would end in divorce. I was afraid of being abandoned.

When I'm angry I feel anxious, nervous, and out of control. I have a difficult time taking a break from the situation to calm down. I often feel extreme pressure to fix the problem immediately.

He yelled at our teenage daughter for anything. He questioned her every move and didn't trust her. One time she talked disrespectfully to him. He got so mad he pushed her down. He did not hurt her physically, but emotionally. I stepped between them and yelled at both of them. I lost it!

At the beginning of all this, my anger was at the military for not taking proper care of my warrior. Then I was angry that he didn't return home with the "woohoo, I'm alive!" attitude. I was angry that he thought his life was over, that he had no future. I'm angry that the military didn't warn me about how my warrior's PTSD would affect me. I'm angry that more isn't being done for the caregivers and the families of our wounded warriors. I'm angry there aren't already support groups in place on every installation around the world. War is not new.

When I am angry, I physically tense up. I feel like my body is about two feet behind my emotions and I'm moving faster than I actually am.

Anger is a slow bleed. It oozes from unattended invisible wounds, our warriors' and our own. Before we can start to heal, we have to recognize and admit that we are deeply angry. Only then can we begin to unravel it, disarm it, and redirect that energy toward something helpful.

Offsetting What Sets Us Off

According to *Women's Health* magazine, 39 percent of women have destroyed something in a rage. And though three out of four of us think it's not all right to go to bed angry, half of us hold grudges. About one-third of us have thrown a punch and almost half of us seek revenge. The top three things that the average woman does to reduce anger is vent to a friend, practice deep breathing, and exercise.[3]

A warrior's hurtful words and actions are not excused, but it helps to know that usually the soft targets are not to blame. Refusing to take your warrior's anger personally is a key step. Part of becoming resilient on the home front is learning to adapt in order to protect ourselves emotionally and physically. A safety buffer begins with a better understanding of the warrior's anger as well as our own.

If there is no resolution to the problem or agitation in the immediate, then the best step we can do is to take care of ourselves. We can't resolve the warrior's issues, so that leaves one option for the here and now: identifying those things that we can affect or control and developing the inner resources to maintain a balance.

I've learned that I do have more options than just blowing up and handing him what he's dealing me. In a recent argument, when things were escalating I stopped the conversation on my end. I saw the argument just circling because neither of us was backing down. So I held my tongue and just said as few words as needed and let my husband do the rest of the talking. The problem wasn't resolved for a few more days, but this did help in minimizing the potential hurt and damage like what used to happen.

I used to start jumping through hoops to try to please him. The more I jumped, the angrier he got, so I don't jump as much these days.

Recently, I noticed he had several "off" days. I asked him if it was an anniversary time for him. He stopped and said, "Oh, yeah. Yes, it is." It is astounding to me that forty-two years after the incident, his body and emotions still carry the traumatic memories and have a profound effect on him.

I find that taking my kids to the park or taking a walk helps to divert my mind from all the tension that is burning when I sit and stew. I read a book or watch a television show or favorite movie. I get counseling when I need it.

Walking, walking, and more walking. I listen to old hymns, not praise music. I rely on "Titus 2" women, mature in their faith, whom God has provided during the worst parts of this journey.

I try to think first before speaking. This is better than saying something I will regret later. Proverbs 15:1 says, "A gentle answer turns away wrath, but a harsh word stirs up anger."

I drove to the church one morning. When my pastor opened the door, I was crying hysterically. I ran to the altar. I felt it was the safest place I could be. I cried for hours, sitting there with my Bible and praying. My pastor's wife spoke with me and we prayed together. She gave me guidance.

I take a brisk walk or a bubble bath or listen to relaxing music, something that is just for me. I can then regroup and assess my thoughts and possible responses to what has happened. I try to find the humor in the situation. I pray and read my Bible.

Exercise and journaling have been the most helpful things I do to keep stress and anger under control. It's okay to relax and just do something for myself. The to-do list doesn't go anywhere if I take some time for self-nurturing.

I call a friend or my prayer partner. I listen to my favorite Christian radio stations. This ministers to me.

Deep breathing low in my belly is very helpful. I try to make my shoulders drop and slow my breathing. I remind myself that God has this. I am not strong enough, but God is. I pour my heart out to Him. He is the only one who truly gets this.

I am grateful for so many blessings and graces given me. I try not to take them for granted. And yet, many days there remains a gnawing anger. I have felt alone in my unrest. I wrestle with surprisingly raw thoughts. I bring them forward, then push them back, way back, deeper, mute them, and try to suffocate them. I know the truth. My best weapon is the peace of God. But at times it rings so hollow and empty to me. God tells me He is my peace. I have known this God and His peace that surpasses all understanding.[4] Yet PTSD brings about an anger darker and deeper than I care to admit. I'm asking Him for a new filling of that peace from the top of my head to the soles of my feet.

Anger is neither right nor wrong. It simply is. "Anger is a signal, and one worth listening to," writes Harriet Lerner, PhD, author of the best-selling *The Dance of Anger: A Woman's Guide to Changing the Patterns of Intimate Relationships*. "Our anger may be a message that we are being hurt, that our rights are being violated, that our needs or wants are not being adequately met, or simply that something is not right. Our anger may tell us that we are not addressing an important emotional issue in our lives, or that too much of our self—our beliefs, values, desires, or ambitions—is being compromised in a relationship. Our anger may be a signal that we are doing more and giving more than we can comfortably do or give. . . . Just as physical pain tells us to take our hand off the hot stove, the pain of our anger preserves the very integrity of our self. Our anger can motivate us to say 'no' to the ways in which we are defined by others and 'yes' to the dictates of our inner self." [5]

God experiences anger. My New Year's resolution a few years ago was to read the Bible from cover to cover. In the first month or so, I breezed along, enjoying the accounts of the creation and stories of Abraham, Isaac, and Jacob and his sons. Wide-eyed, I eagerly traveled through the exciting scenes of God freeing the Israelites from Egypt and splitting the sea for their sandals to stay dry as they left the land of their slavery forever. Sometime around March my journey through the Scriptures became more difficult as I encountered books like Leviticus, and later, Isaiah, Jeremiah, and Ezekiel. I was no longer at a comfortable cruising altitude. I hung on for dear life as in chapter after chapter the writers described in detail the terrible anger of Almighty God. Day after day, I leaned into the winds of His wrath and trudged forward, determined to reach my goal by year's end. There were many days I had to take a detour into the New Testament, gasping for grace!

If God is holy, and He is, then anger can be expressed in a right way. It is a God-given emotion. We have a choice what we do with it. The moment anger awakens, we must discern whether its motive is to preserve the best and guard the welfare of that which God values or whether its motive is the preservation of me, myself, and mine. If anger's motive is right in God's eyes, then we can pray for His help and grace in carefully expressing it without sinning.[6]

The following are helpful questions to ask ourselves when we experience anger:

- Can I identify why I am angry?
- With whom am I angry?
- Is this the best place to express my anger?
- Do I have any options right now?

I am learning to take a deep breath, to look around and head toward the space that I am sure belongs to me. I am learning to recognize those things over which I have control, those personal spaces in which my key fits. Once I understood my husband's and son's withdrawal and distancing as a warrior-club thing, I was better able to respond to the changes at home and in family relationships. I was then able to add a phrase to my email signature without bitterness, but with a smile: *Joshua was recently awarded the Bronze Star for Valor for things sons don't tell their mothers.* I am very proud of our son, even if I don't have all the details.

Questions for Reflection

1. Have you seen signs of anger in your warrior? If so, describe how he/she has expressed anger at home and in interaction with you and other family members.

2. Have you experienced feelings of anger in response to your warrior's displays of irritability, annoyance, rage, or self-destructive choices? Tell about a situation that caused you to feel anger.

3. When you feel angry in relation to your warrior, are you able to identify specifically *why* you are angry? In the situation you described above, at whom or at what were you angry?

4. How do you know when you are angry? Describe your physical and mental condition when you are angry.

5. Our response to anger can cause us problems. In your struggle to deal with your anger, have you ever said or done anything you regretted? Describe one *inappropriate* choice (harmful to self or others) you've made while angry. What life lesson did you learn from it?

6. Our response to anger can help us. In your struggle to deal with your anger, have you ever responded in a healthy, God-honoring way? Share one *appropriate* choice (helpful, redirecting, alternative) you've made while angry. What life lesson did you learn from taking this approach?

7. What have you found to be most helpful in redirecting or resolving your anger? (Physical exercise/activities, specific Scripture verses, relaxation techniques, hobbies, counseling, etc.)

4

Smelly Issues and the Fragrance of Forgiveness

For we are to God the pleasing aroma of Christ among those who are being saved and those who are perishing.

2 Corinthians 2:15

*E*very pipe in our house was backed up. The stale August night air trapped the stench indoors and turned our home into a smelly sauna. We were rearing three kids under five years old on one military salary and a bank account that gasped for life between paychecks. Our choices were few. We could grab the kids and the photo albums and run or we could stand, breathe through our mouths, and fight. Mark fearlessly faced the enemy, plunging toilets and tubs as I tried to locate an after-hours plumber.

He arrived just in time. I took the kids next door and entrusted our problem to Mark and the plumber, who graciously offered us a deal: If Mark would help him dig down to the four-inch main in the front yard, he would give us a generous discount. Mark gladly grabbed his shovel and sank its sharp edge into the damp, grassy earth. He dug in the dark while I rocked our three rug rats to sleep in our neighbor's recliner.

Somewhere between midnight and morning, the expensive mole unearthed the culprit. "The plumber always knows" was his only comment as he pulled the plug from the pipe: a wad of Waddell panties. As he untangled a knotted parade of Disney undies including soiled Cinderella, Beauty and the Beast, and Winnie the Pooh, the truth was revealed. Apparently, our pig-tailed toddler's potty training had taken a turn for the worse. Jordan, our first daughter, had figured out she could flush the evidence before anyone knew she had made a mess.

Before she was busted, the bounce in Jordan's step and the sparkle in her blue eyes had us all fooled. All indicators pointed to an unprecedented potty training victory. Meanwhile the subterranean evidence silently gnarled itself into an impasse. Outwardly she beamed with newfound confidence; inwardly she privately wrestled with her personal failures.

Forgiveness on the Home Front

In an environment in which everyone involved is always waiting for the next eruption, some serious soul-searching is in order. We who love and live with a combat veteran desperately desire the wholeness of our loved one and the restoration of our most cherished relationships.

Forgiveness is an important step toward hope and healing on the home front—the forgiveness we need from the Father for our own sins, the forgiveness we give ourselves, and the forgiveness we extend to others. There are no shortcuts. Our journey toward embracing our new normal, moving forward and rebuilding in the aftermath of war, must inevitably intersect with God's command to "[forgive] each other, just as in Christ God forgave you."[1] Our personal healing and, consequently, the healing of our relationships and homes, begins with forgiveness, the forgiveness God offers to us and the forgiveness He requires us to offer to ourselves and to others.

I started this chapter by sharing with you some of our family's dirty laundry in order to highlight the importance of dealing with one's own sins first.[2] Whether our poor choices are intentionally kept hidden or we simply haven't identified the source of the stench yet, Jesus' challenge remains the same: "If any one of you is without sin, let him be the first to throw a stone. . . ."[3] In other words, acknowledge first your own sin.

The list of offenses against you may be long, but I urge you to start with addressing your own sins. This will lead to a critical truth: we can fully obey God's command to forgive others' sins against us *only* when we have asked for, received, and experienced God's undeserved, gracious, merciful forgiveness of our failures first. This life-changing experience births a heart that pulses with thankfulness out of which we can genuinely—and supernaturally—extend and demonstrate God's grace to our debtors. There's no other order, I believe, in the process of true forgiveness. When we realize the incalculable riches and decadent pardon God has lavished on us, we are quicker to cancel any debts owed to us in relationships on the home front.

Bottom line, we can't forgive others until we realize how much God has forgiven us through His Son's sacrifice, the only offering that turns away God's wrath that we fully deserve. This is the truest, most noble, most admirable, loveliest, most praiseworthy thought I can have in any given moment. When I stop to think on this, even for just a few seconds, I feel my heart swell, expand, and take on a greater capacity to forgive others.

Father, Forgive Us Our Sins

None of us has handled the challenges of PTSD on the home front with perfection. All of us have either willfully or unwittingly responded to combat stress in ways that miss the mark. You may be thinking, *I know what I did or said was wrong, but considering my situation I had every right to do such and such or to feel this or that way.*

Regardless of rationale, we have all fallen short of what God expects of us. Not that we disappointed God, though. That's impossible. Disappointment houses an element of surprise by definition, and because we can't ever surprise God, we don't ever disappoint Him, technically. He knew from the foundation of the world where, when, and how we would flub up. The great news is He provided the means for our forgiveness—Jesus Christ's death on the cross—long before we took our first breath.

It's been said that conscience is what hurts when everything else feels so good. Let's revisit the panties and the backed-up sewer main. Remember the bounce in our daughter's step and the sparkle in her blue eyes that had us all fooled?

Before I got honest with myself and with the Lord about stuff that was clogging my spiritual pipes, I, too, had a bounce in my step and a sparkle in my blue eyes that had everyone around me fooled for a while. At a low point in my marriage, I found ways to hide the truth from myself and others—and chose some damaging ways to do it. I was convinced that I could keep the truth from view. After a while, everything percolated to the top. When I spewed, spiritually speaking, everyone got to enjoy the stench for a while.

The Mess in the Mirror

I asked God to forgive me, which He did right away as promised.[4] I asked my family to forgive me, which they did, but not right away. The hardest part was forgiving myself. I disgusted me. I couldn't stand the sound of my own voice or the sight of myself in the mirror for the mess I had made.

Why do we joyfully lap up forgiveness from God and welcome it with tears from others, but then hesitate or outright refuse to offer it to ourselves? God's Word tells us that He instantly pardons the sin of the sincere, repentant heart. Why don't we? Do we doubt our own sincerity? We let everyone but ourselves off the hook. How can we justify withholding forgiveness from ourselves when God has already fully picked up our tab? What does our hesitancy or refusal to forgive ourselves say about our heart of hearts and about our view of God's gift of mercy? May I suggest that it says we subconsciously consider ourselves holier than God and, therefore, our forgiveness standard can be set a few notches higher than His.

The apostle Paul, carried along by the Holy Spirit, directed us to "bear with each other and forgive whatever grievances you may have against one another. Forgive as the Lord forgave you."[5] That includes the grievances we have against *ourselves*. God wants us to forgive ourselves even as the Lord forgave us. I encourage you to offer yourself at least the same measure of grace and patience that you repeatedly and readily offer to your warrior and to your family members every day. Simply and sincerely ask God to help you fully forgive yourself and move forward.

As We Forgive Those Who Sin against Us

The frequency and the severity of offenses experienced in the home wracked by combat stress have few equals in the civilian realm. The invisible injuries combat veterans and their family members intentionally or unintentionally cause one another call for a greater urgency to understand the priority forgiveness must have in healing the home front.

Wives, mothers, and children of combat veterans are deeply wounded by their warriors' denial of any problem, his avoidance of the topic, and his lies and half-truths. Wrongful blaming of others and name-calling cut deeply. Families pay the high price for the inevitable emotional roller coaster when their veterans decide to supervise their own health care and manage their own prescribed medications. Wives frequently report emotional and physical infidelity on the veteran's part and the hurtful rejection and loss of intimacy that follows. Family members are wounded by their warriors' alcohol or drug abuse and other addictive or risky behaviors. They share their struggles to forgive extended family members for their words and actions that stem from a lack of understanding about military life, combat stress, post-traumatic stress disorder, and traumatic brain injury. They tire of the seven-times-seventy standard of forgiveness which Jesus set for us in Luke 17:4. Jesus' command to offer forgiveness to our brother "times without number" (NIV footnote) seems outrageous. And just when the situation seems to stabilize somewhat, memories of the offense are triggered. The emotions that were a part of the original event return full force, skipping right alongside the flashback, and cause us to doubt whether we ever truly forgave in the first place.

I have let go of all the words, the hurtful words flung at me in the past. The digs, the threats, the assassinations and crucifixions done with words. I am told and I want to believe that those words no longer have power over me, over my present, over my future. Yet, I remember those words. They echo. They return. Can the words echo and still be powerless? Can I be healed of their hurt, yet still remember every intonation and every facial expression that accompanied the words? They do not sleep. Yet I am to believe I am healed of their injury and released from their control. Perhaps it will be a slow healing over many days and months and years.

I am not sure it counts as forgiveness if I still struggle with many of these issues. There have been many times when I make the choice to forgive and I feel like I am at peace with everything for long periods of time. Then something

inevitably triggers me to feel as if I have not made any prog-
ress in the last few years. This leaves me wondering if I have
truly forgiven. I have made some conscious choices. I don't
bring up and rehash the past situations to him. I try to always
remember to take my thoughts captive and give them to God
before I try to wrestle them on my own.

Jim Scott, my best friend's father and my second dad, once told me that without forgiveness we plow without rain. He said not forgiving others and myself would be a chain around me, that there would be no successful outcome without forgiveness. All of the therapy sessions, prayer vigils, support groups, and self-help books combined would not be able to free my soul if it were held captive by the lack of forgiveness. He warned me up front that this would be the hardest part of the healing process for my marriage and my family. He said it would be impossible without the help of the Holy Spirit. And then with a sparkle in his crystal blue eyes, he encouraged me, "For nothing is impossible with God."[6]

Think about your veteran and your family as you read the following quotes from women who have walked miles and miles in your shoes.

He has filled our home with fits of rage more times than I
would like to remember. He has fought really dirty by being
verbally and emotionally abusive time and time again.

He has been emotionally unfaithful with other women on
many occasions. He seemed to have only one method of com-
municating with me . . . lying. He smoked marijuana and had
an affair with another woman.

He punched my arm in a fit of rage. He drank excessively
over a three-year period and drove home drunk.

He gave such hurtful looks at me; it still hurts just recalling him looking at me that way.

Communication is so hard. There is this long list of subjects we cannot discuss . . . mostly his PTSD, our marriage, feelings, relationships, especially the family members who don't understand PTSD, our communication, finances . . . all the important stuff. Then there is the list of things we cannot do. All of these things have caused deep hurt and the stress has not ended.

When I made intimate advances he always pushed me away. His rejection hurt me so badly. It still does. After many rejections I told him when he was ready to let me know. I have waited for nearly five years. It is still unbearable to be left in limbo, waiting for him to want me as his wife again.

The offense I've found to be the most difficult to forgive? Hands down . . . my warrior pushing me out of our marriage, his not wanting to work through all this together.

The hardest things for me have been the infidelity, the lying, and the drunkenness.

I think the hardest part was dealing with parents and grandparents. They were so against him going into the service in the first place and continually tried to do everything in their power to convince us to get out. When he came home wounded, I had to try to explain what I didn't understand myself. Relationships were stressed in the process. I had to forgive them for trying to protect us and give them mercy for not being able to ever understand. It wasn't their fault, but it tested all of our immediate relationships.

I still haven't forgiven him for joining the military without any real input from me. And then, I haven't forgiven myself for not forgiving him!

Our purpose in sharing bluntly isn't to whine or warrior-bash. We addressed our own sins as first priority. Our hearts' desire is that transparency will help you to realize you are not alone.

True, without forgiveness, we plow without rain—all of our other efforts will be unproductive and pointless. I have discovered that an unforgiving heart toward my warrior always ends up hurting me the most and never brings about the peace, justice, or restitution I crave. And this lack of forgiveness propels us to find peace elsewhere, as if that were possible. So we venture away from our families and marriages, but instead of finding peace, we end up filling the emptiness in unhealthy ways that also keep us out of fellowship with the Father.[7]

Pastor and author Charles Stanley points out that lack of forgiveness can blind us to the way God sees us and others.[8] Lack of forgiveness is a seed of hatred with immeasurable potential for harm. "Anyone who claims to be in the light but hates his brother is still in the darkness. Whoever loves his brother lives in the light, and there is nothing in him to make him stumble. But whoever hates his brother is in the darkness and walks around in the darkness; he does not know where he is going, because the darkness has blinded him."[9]

Lack of forgiveness produces an unwillingness to love others which prevents us from loving the Lord with our whole being. "If anyone says, 'I love God,' yet hates his brother, he is a liar. For anyone who does not love his brother, whom he has seen, cannot love God, whom he has not seen. And he has given us this command: Whoever loves God must also love his brother."[10]

We can safely say that forgiveness is helpful and that refusing to forgive not only blocks good health and healing but can cause more harm to others and to ourselves. So, if forgiveness is the key to maintaining our spiritual plumbing, let's begin to dig down in order to bring our sins into the light. Forgiveness is the cancellation of a debt owed to you. This could be a debt of trust, a debt of intimacy, a debt of honor and respect. The word forgive is a verb, an action word, something we do, not something we feel. William P. Young, author of *The Shack*, defined forgiveness as releasing the death grip you have on the offender's proverbial throat.

Wash Day

I've finally learned God's pattern. He doesn't allow me to advise, counsel, or encourage others on any topic unless He first leads me through the same or a similar valley. I can be sure that if I've been invited to write or speak on any given topic, I had better prepare myself for a big dose of that very theme unfolding in my life before that date. If I've been asked to speak about the virtue of patience, for example, I may as well write "intense, painful testing of my patience" on my calendar in a red Sharpie on the thirty days preceding that event. If I've been invited to be a guest blogger and to contribute a post about how military couples can communicate better, I immediately start bracing myself for imminent communication meltdowns in my marriage. I shouldn't have been surprised that as I settled in to write a chapter for this book about forgiveness, that I'd first have to practice what I preach before God would hand me the pen.

At Hope for the Home Front, one of our main objectives during the "When War Comes Home *Don't* Retreat" weekend conferences is to help wives, mothers, and daughters of combat veterans with PTSD to discern between those things they can affect, influence, change, or control, like their hair color and wardrobe, and those things that they cannot. Kidding. Seriously, we want to help these women identify the changes, small and large, they can make in their lifestyles, choices, and environments, and then to create a personal plan for physical, mental, and spiritual health that incorporates those changes. We emphasize that the first and most important change any family member of a traumatized person can make in choosing personal wholeness is to give and to receive forgiveness for all hurts on the home front.

The hurts on my home front had hurled our marriage against the wall. After my trip to Arizona, Mark and I did not live together for a period of time and the unresolved issues escalated to an all-time high. I felt I had done everything that was within my power to do. In my heart, in the privacy of my own conversations with God, I had forgiven my warrior and myself as best as I understood forgiveness. Yet during one quiet morning with the Lord I clearly sensed that forgiveness without expression was incomplete. While I was reading in the book of Isaiah, suddenly the scene described in John 13 popped into my head, where Jesus washes the feet of His disciples. At the end of the passage, Jesus says,

> "Do you understand what I have done for you?" he asked them.
> "You call me 'Teacher' and 'Lord,' and rightly so, for that is what
> I am. Now that I, your Lord and Teacher, have washed your feet,
> you also should wash one another's feet. I have set you an example
> that you should do as I have done for you. Very truly I tell you, no
> servant is greater than his master, nor is a messenger greater than
> the one who sent him. Now that you know these things, you will
> be blessed if you do them."[11]

I asked the Lord about this, concerned that the leap from Isaiah to John might just be a mild form of ADHD. I instantly knew the next thing to do. I knew how to outwardly express the forgiveness I felt in my heart: Go to Mark and wash his feet as Jesus did in John 13.

Wash his feet, the reply came again.

I headed into my long list of errands, but the prompting to go *wash his feet* continued to enter my thoughts throughout the day.

"Lord, this is nuts," I said out loud in my car. "He will think I've totally lost it. And besides, this marriage is over. Too much damage has been done."

Wash his feet.

"Lord, he has filed for divorce already with the county court. I'm afraid to go do that."

Wash his feet.

In faith, I texted Mark and asked if I could come by his apartment that evening for a very brief visit. He texted back, "Yes."

Prayed up, I showed up with basin, water pitcher, hand towel, and Bible. I knocked. He opened the door. We exchanged awkward, tentative hellos.

"What are you doing?" he asked, looking at the unusual items in my arms. I didn't answer.

I set the empty basin at the foot of his favorite chair and filled the pitcher with warm water. I asked him to sit in the chair and if I could remove his shoes and socks.

"No, you don't have to do this."

"Yes, I do. The Lord has told me to do it."

Quiet and curious, he sat back and tried to relax. I opened my Bible and read the first section of John 13 to him, then closed the book. I washed one foot at a time and dried them with the towel. I laid my hands on his warm, clean feet and prayed aloud that God would enable Mark to stand firm and to honor God in all his choices and decisions. I lightly kissed both of his feet, stood up, and left his apartment. I had been in his presence for twelve minutes.

Numb, but totally at peace, I drove back to my place knowing that I had obeyed God. I had no agenda that night, but God apparently did. I knew I could trust Him to use it for His purposes in our teetering marriage. The next morning, Mark texted me, saying that what I had done "was the most precious experience of being honored that he had ever known." Over the next three days, we experienced breakthroughs in our efforts to communicate, arrived at some solutions to our most pressing issues, and agreed to spend more time together to get reacquainted. Two months later, we were living under the same roof again, and Mark had officially withdrawn the divorce petition from the court system. I'm convinced that by listening to God's lead and following through on His mysterious, quiet demonstration of unconditional love, a foundation of forgiveness paved the way for healing to begin.

I've often wondered about the period of silence that takes place before we finally can forgive, and also about God's silence while we struggle to forgive. Actually, the silence of God is a signal that something significant is about to take place. Whether or not our story ends well depends on what we do while God is silent. In the quiet, we have a choice to cling to His promises or to grow cold to them. God was silent for four hundred years between Malachi and Matthew. I can't imagine enduring four centuries without a peep from heaven. I want to know that even now, even in my bleakest moment, even when I am spiritually rotten and offensive to all those around me, God can show up on my darkest day and rescue me from the cemetery of my own deadly decisions.

God says that my strength is in quietness and trust.[12] I may not see or hear Him at work, but because He promised to never leave me,[13] I believe He is close by and fully engaged. The Prince of Peace is also a plumber. In the silence that I wrongly interpret as His desertion, disinterest, or disgust, He is up to His elbows in my front yard rooting around for the problem in my spiritual pipes that needs unplugging.

Jesus' silence before His accusers came just before He pulled the plug on the whole world's sins. His blood that flowed removed the barriers that block our knowledge of and our service to our living God. That incredible news gives us the strength we need to forgive—again.

Questions for Reflection

1. Do you have a favorite definition of forgiveness or a favorite quote about forgiveness? If so, share it along with its source.

2. What are some of the debts your warrior has run up against you since he returned home from combat? What are some of the things he has done that have hurt or offended you (or your kids) that call for forgiveness?

3. Which offense or hurt have you found to be the most difficult to forgive?

4. In what ways have you injured your warrior and/or your children either by words or actions? Be honest.

5. If you have not fully forgiven your warrior or yourself, do you see how unoffered forgiveness or smoldering resentment might be affecting your **physical** health? If so, how?

   Do you see how unoffered forgiveness or smoldering resentment might be affecting your **mental** health and balance? If so, how?

   Do you see how unoffered forgiveness or smoldering resentment might be affecting your **spiritual** health and growth? If so, how?

6. If you honestly feel you have forgiven your warrior and yourself for that offense/debt, what are some of the steps you took to work through the process of forgiveness?

5

Weary, Worn Out, and Wondering Why

> Then, because so many people were coming and going that they did not even have a chance to eat, he said to them, "Come with me by yourselves to a quiet place and get some rest."
>
> Mark 6:31

This place has a beauty all its own," my husband commented to me somewhere between Devils River and Big Satan Creek. Shocked, I shot a sideways glance at him to make sure he wasn't sleep-talking at the wheel. *Certainly he must be in some sort of trance or stupor*, I thought, *if he considers this stretch of Interstate 10 beautiful*. We were driving between El Paso and Fort Worth. Three tortuous hours earlier, the woman who lives inside my GPS had told us to drive 589 miles before preparing to make a right turn. Hundreds of miles of blacktop still lay ahead of us, a dark gray ribbon ironed flat by West Texas heat. Why would anyone ever choose to live in this seemingly barren parcel of earth? The stinging thought of having to write a West Texas zipcode in my return address for the rest of my life was repulsive.

This area of West Texas, scientists tell us, used to be covered in water, a vast sea teeming with life. It made me wonder: How does an ocean up and leave? How do powerful swells, deep waters, and crashing waves just wander off to distant lands? Did the seams of her ocean floor stretch too far and split ever so slightly? Did she spring a small leak that caused all breath and beauty to trickle away, until her shriveled seabed lay eerily silent? In any case, the ocean was gone now and all that was left behind was a gaping shell.

Twenty-five years of U.S. Navy life had anchored us in lush, desirable duty stations like San Diego, Hawaii, Virginia Beach, and the Republic of Panama, where each day brimmed with life, energy, and light. Our hearts and our hopes teemed with life then too. Now the fears we faced, the pace we kept, and the immeasurable losses we took stirred our waters violently and our marriage and family were stretched past capacity. We had hairline cracks in our foundation, and as they slowly opened, our life together drained away. Our family, that had loved and lived in lush, tropical places of mind, body, and soul before war, now wrote a desert zipcode as our psychological and spiritual return address.

Mile Markers

I glanced at the GPS: 394 dull miles to go. I began to mentally reconstruct the road between what had been the condition of my heart at the start of the war and the shriveled state I find it in now a decade later, between a place of believing I could weather any storm to this place of total burnout.

In the process, I identified a dozen mile markers on the imaginary interstate where the starting line had been faith and unflinching determination and the finish line is fatigue and a persistent emotional flatness. I share these twelve warning signs to help you evaluate your own journey. If you pass any of these markers, stop the journey. Pull off the highway and begin the process of turning around. Each represents a place for you to exit the highway that leads to burnout, an opportunity for you to make a *you*-turn toward improved physical and mental health.

Mile Marker 1: I was determined, even compelled, to prove myself at the outset of my husband's first and, later, our son's first combat deployments. I felt a surge of ambition, resolve, and commitment not only to endure but to triumph, come what may.

Mile Marker 2: When my husband returned from his first combat deployment with a broken leg, I rolled up my sleeves and worked harder than ever, taking on more responsibility than usual. During the deployments, and oddly even after my husband returned, I became obsessed with handling everything by myself, without asking for assistance. I was making myself, I believed, indispensable.

Mile Marker 3: Several deployments later, with a PTSD diagnosis added to my husband's challenges, I had zero time for anything that resembled relaxation. I prided myself as I strived to attain a Proverbs 31 standard of what makes a woman approved and valuable, rising at the crack of dawn and working way past bedtime to fulfill my many goals to be a tireless wife, award-winning mom, loyal friend, ready volunteer, and nice neighbor. I crossed off my list anything and anyone outside the realm of what felt productive.

Mile Marker 4: I began to sense that I was off balance physically, emotionally, and spiritually, but I was unwilling to invest the time or energy required to recalibrate. I began to pull away from my closest relationships. After taking care of the needs around me around the clock, I had nothing left to invest in others. In an effort to protect myself and my mission, I isolated. I found an island and stayed there.

Mile Marker 5: I began to ignore my basic needs. When I felt sleepy, I forced myself to stay awake and keep working. When my head hurt, I pretended it didn't. When my stomach growled, I teased it with mini meals or tortured it with fatty foods and other poor nutritional choices. When my children made requests, I barked at them. When my close girlfriends expressed concern for me, I blew them away with my bluntness. My time with God shrank. I quit attending women's Bible studies and only sporadically attended Sunday worship services.

Mile Marker 6: Doing anything that included interaction with others became intolerable. My closest friends gently tried to tell me that I was becoming sarcastic and aggressive, that I had changed. But I was convinced that I hadn't changed, *they* had. *Everyone* had changed, but me.

Mile Marker 7: I started smoking again. I had hidden the habit from my parents in high school. Now I found myself hiding it from my adult children. I began to drink socially after fifteen self-righteous dry years. Then I began to drink alone. I felt hopeless and burdened by the belief that life for our family would never improve. I lacked clear direction.

Mile Marker 8: My closest ones told me that they could no longer ignore the changes they saw in me. They encouraged me to "get help," to find a trustworthy professional counselor and an emotionally safe environment where I could regularly drop off the baggage. How could I get help for my issues, I responded, when I was busy helping everyone else carry theirs?

Mile Marker 9: I felt that I was just going through the motions each day. Every day was drudgery. I felt disconnected from my own head and heart. I couldn't find me anymore.

Mile Marker 10: I felt empty inside, so I began to look for ways to fill that emptiness. My list did not include healthy options, but only risky, self-destructive ones.

Mile Marker 11: The demands of repeated deployments and the mounting unresolved aftermath of combat on the home front shut down my peripheral vision. I became convinced that this was all there is, that there was nothing ahead to look forward to anymore. I resigned myself to a life of exhaustion, disappointment, and indifference.

Mile Marker 12: I contemplated death. I toyed with thoughts of the life hereafter and looked for painless ways to get there.

I had arrived at the end of my rope. I had ignored the telltale signs that told me my life was on a collision course between the needs of my body, soul, and mind and my self-induced schedule. I am grateful I finally listened to the trustworthy advice of concerned friends, family members, and trained professionals who helped me to correct my coordinates and find a better way to care for my wounded warrior and myself.

Lapse, Relapse, and Collapse

According to Patricia Smith and the Compassion Fatigue Awareness Project, "Caring too much can hurt. . . . One form of Secondary Traumatic Stress is feeling burned out, officially known as 'Compassion Fatigue.' Compassion Fatigue is not a disease. It is the natural result of prolonged stress from caring for and helping traumatized people or animals."[1] A person who is experiencing serious burnout is in a state of mental and physical collapse caused by overwork or chronic stress. She displays most or all of the following symptoms:

Excessive blaming

Bottled-up emotions

Isolation from others

Receives unusual number of complaints

Voices excessive complaints

Substance abuse used to mask feelings

Compulsive behaviors (overspending, overeating, gambling, sexual addictions)

Poor self-care (hygiene, appearance)

Legal problems, indebtedness

Nightmares, flashbacks to traumatic event

Chronic physical ailments (digestive, respiratory, and achiness)

Apathy, sad, no longer finds activities pleasurable

Difficulty concentrating

Mentally and physically tired

Preoccupied

In denial about problems[2]

Compassion Fatigue can be caused by:

Placing the needs of others before your own

Unresolved past trauma and pain in your life

A lack of healthy communication skills

A lack of awareness of your basic needs for growth and health

An inability to communicate your needs

Refusal or hesitation to ask for assistance

An absence of personal boundaries, inability to say no

A chronic need to prove yourself to others

The demands of a dysfunctional relationship

A lack of restful sleep and enjoyable activities[3]

Burnout on the Home Front

Spouses and family members of combat veterans report that the biggest reasons for burnout on the home front are placing the needs of others before their own combined with a refusal or hesitation to ask for help, the demands of a dysfunctional relationship, and a lack of restful sleep.

I feel extremely impatient, worn out, resentful, unappreciated. I need energy to cope. I have a rapid heartbeat. I pray to God: Why me, Lord? Please not another day of coping with PTSD!

After taking care of my husband for an extended period of time, having everything to see to, I recall a certain day when I was irritated at everybody in my path. I couldn't even speak kindly. It seemed that I couldn't control myself! I barked at some man in the grocery store and I don't remember why.

I take care of myself last. I become short of temper or quiet because I am imploding. I feel as though I haven't slept in three days, carrying everyone's burden on myself and going non-stop.

I was doing what I thought I should be doing—taking care of my warrior. The thought of doing something for myself seemed selfish. I would quickly refocus my attention on him. The demands of this new dysfunctional relationship kept me running on empty daily. I never knew just what I was supposed to be doing. I just did what I thought had to be done. With no directions included, I just flew by the seat of my pants.

I become so stressed out and tired that anything my husband and children do that wouldn't normally get on my nerves becomes a huge deal and makes me want to pull out my hair.

The constant drain caused restless sleep. Pretty soon, my body and mind had had enough. I was exhausted in every way. Enjoyable activities? What are those? The first few years there were none. Even when I did try to do something fun, I did not enjoy it at all. My mind was worrying about tasks needing to be done. I went through the motions, but I felt no joy in them.

I know I'm dealing with compassion fatigue because I become impatient with my loved ones. I tend to cry very easily. I start having feelings of hopelessness, which is not reflective of the real me.

As family members and close friends of returning warriors, we naturally place their needs before our own. We have fiercely missed them, faithfully prayed for them, and are forever grateful they are home relatively safe. We are proud of their service and wish to honor their sacrifices. We hurt when they hurt and look for ways to reduce or eliminate their physical or emotional pain. When PTSD surfaces on the home front, these desires become intensified, muddled, and layered. As the daily chores and relational responsibilities at home increase, instead of asking for help from others, we don our superhero cape and try to tackle everything solo. Why not? We handled it all on our own while our service member was deployed. We do so partly because we want to prove to ourselves and to others that we are capable, but also because we are peacemaking. Subconsciously or consciously we try to cover for our loved one's unpredictable, asymmetric response to different situations. We don't wish to dishonor or upset our warrior by bringing outsiders into the mix. Isolating and overextending ourselves create a ripe environment for further dysfunction in our relationship with our warrior, our children, and our extended family. We keep our lives in overdrive for so long that we forget how to slow down, relax, and sleep soundly. Our nights are fitful with short cycles of restless sleep hyphenated by tossing, turning, and keeping one eye on our warrior.

Compassion fatigue and burnout are not unique to families who love and live with a combat veteran. Neither are they exclusive to one era or area of the world. The white flag of fatigue has been flown in every life, regardless of generation or culture, since Adam and Eve left Eden. Some of the Bible's biggest spiritual giants found themselves running out of steam too. King David desperately wanted to escape the demands of his life. "I said, 'Oh, that I had the wings of a dove! I would fly away and be at rest.'"[4] Job, who God himself described as righteous, had reached the end of his righteous rope when he said, "I despise my life; I would not live forever. Let me alone; my days have no meaning."[5] Solomon, known as the wisest man who ever lived, also experienced the emptiness of burnout: "All their days their work is grief and pain; even at night their minds do not rest. This too is meaningless."[6] Be encouraged; you are in great company.

Red, Right, Returning: The Road to Recovery

Professionals agree that the first step toward recovering from compassion fatigue and burnout is learning how to recognize and manage the symptoms. The rough road that leads from beautiful to burned-out can feel longer and look bleaker than my drive on Interstate 10. The great news is that burnout doesn't have to be a dead end. Thankfully, it's a road with lots of turn lanes that allow us to pull over and slow down, to stop and sightsee for a spell, or to look both ways, do a *you*-turn, and head in the other direction.

The Compassion Fatigue Awareness Project has compiled some helpful steps you can take to break the draining cycle of Compassion Fatigue:

Accept that the situation *itself* is stressful.

Share your feelings with a trusted friend, co-worker, or trusted family member.

Listen to others and acknowledge their perspective about the situation.

Enhance your communication skills with your warrior and with your family.

Improve your anger-management skills.

Take positive action to change your daily environment.

Exercise good time management. Learn how to distinguish between needs and wants.

Commit to daily physical exercise.

Commit to regular counseling and improving mental health.

Commit to strengthening faith and improving spiritual health.

Listen to your body and practice healthy self-care.

Take time away from your stressful situation. Make a date with yourself weekly and replenish your mind and soul.

Allow others to help you.[7]

The home front leads toward health when those closest to the warrior apply this wisdom and diligently follow through each day. The result is a renewed mind and recharged strength for the journey.

I accept that the situation is stressful. I manage my stress and seek the support of family, friends, and even of my wounded warrior. I replenish my mind spiritually, commit to physical exercise. I work at not overextending myself. By saying "no," I can say "yes" to the things I really want to do.

Burnout can be an opportunity to rediscover what really makes me happy and to change the course of my life accordingly.

We have developed different ways of communicating more effectively. By having a few simple communication rules, life is easier day by day. Taking time for myself when I need it allows me to be stronger for myself and for my family.

When my husband first started experiencing PTSD, I worried that I would stubbornly stick it out and not know appropriate boundaries. I wavered back and forth with my thoughts, not sure who I really was. I praised myself for being committed, strong, faithful, and enduring. I worried that I would repeat unhealthy behaviors I observed in my own family of origin. I've come a long way. I couldn't do it without God.

Accepting that our entire existence has been altered is a huge step in itself. When daily stressors emerge, they are handled more appropriately. It has been a great help to talk with a friend who gets it. I journal when I'm really stressed and can't or don't want to vent verbally. I talk to God and vent to Him quite often. I know He is really the only one who completely gets it.

I found that it helped me to have my loved one in the presence of other loved ones (family) who genuinely cared for my husband. Their presence helped share the load and gave me some space.

I committed to regular counseling for more than a year. I still go occasionally. This helped me learn coping techniques I would have never known to apply.

With help we get past this exhaustion, exasperation, the just-one-more-expectation, the just-one-more-need somebody has. We become able to move away from the present (if only temporarily) and to get a breather and another beginning. Just enough energy will come to strengthen us for today . . . and tomorrow.

Six simple practices help to heal and to revive our minds, bodies, and spirits. They include committing to regular physical exercise, maintaining a healthy diet, making time for enjoyable social activities, journaling or doing other forms of creative expression, and restful sleep. These five daily steps are the manna for overcoming the monotony of caregiving. However, they are temporary fixes. They are bandages we stick on the burnout. Because we are frail and finite, even a faithful commitment to this five-part recipe for resilience leaves us fatigued and feeling hopeless. It lacks the most important—sixth—ingredient.

Wellness from the Well

I took a spoonful of my own medicine last week by making *and keeping* a date with myself. I visited a local art museum. For a couple hours, my eyes feasted on visual delights that included Monet, Van Gogh, and Caravaggio. None captivated me more than an early seventeenth-century painting by an Italian artist named Guercino. *Christ and the Woman of Samaria* captured my full attention. I immediately loved the rich palette the artist had chosen, and his ability to depict the figures and scenery with such detailed realism.

After a few moments of politely gazing at the painting, I turned away to take several steps toward the next masterpiece, but didn't get far. For reasons that were not yet clear to me, my heart was tethered to *Christ and the Woman of Samaria*. I did an about-face and re-engaged with the painting. After a few seconds, I realized that it wasn't the artist's hues and handiwork that demanded my focus as much as his intent and message. The painting seemed to speak to me personally.

Jesus and the unnamed woman are alone at the well, He on our left and she on our right. She rests her arms on the empty bucket she has set on the lip of Jacob's well. His disciples are nowhere to be found. Neither have any other women come with her to draw water. Jesus and the woman have one another's undivided attention. Her shadowed face is turned toward His as she listens to Him speak to her. Their eye contact is tender and intense. He is in midsentence, sharing something her heart desperately needs to hear.

My recollection of the New Testament account of the woman at the well had dried up from nonuse. Although I had read it at least a hundred times, I couldn't remember it fully. I couldn't get home quickly enough to reread the rich details of the story. I was positive that the Artist behind the art was offering me a cool drink. As soon as I could get alone with my Bible, I turned to the book of John, chapter 4.

Jesus and His disciples were on their way north to His home turf in Galilee. In order to get there, He chose to travel through Samaria, the land of what Jews considered filthy crossbred squatters. The racism kept Jews in one lane and the Samaritans in the other. Ne'er the twain met, except on rare occasions of the God-ordained variety. John tells us that because Jesus was tired, He stopped at the well near Sychar. At high noon, a Samaritan woman arrived with her water jar.

> When a Samaritan woman came to draw water, Jesus said to her, "Will you give me a drink?" (His disciples had gone into the town to buy food.)
>
> The Samaritan woman said to him, "You are a Jew and I am a Samaritan woman. How can you ask me for a drink?" (For Jews do not associate with Samaritans.)

Jesus answered her, "If you knew the gift of God and who it is that asks you for a drink, you would have asked him and he would have given you living water."

"Sir," the woman said, "you have nothing to draw with and the well is deep. Where can you get this living water? Are you greater than our father Jacob, who gave us the well and drank from it himself, as did also his sons and his livestock?"

Jesus answered, "Everyone who drinks this water will be thirsty again, but whoever drinks the water I give them will never thirst. Indeed, the water I give them will become in them a spring of water welling up to eternal life."[8]

Our girlfriend south of Galilee had kept the home fires burning not for one, but for *five* husbands. After number five, she burned out and defaulted to simply shacking up with beau number six. Each dull day she must have felt that she was just going through the motions. Not only were her former friends nowhere to be found, but she couldn't even find herself anymore. Convinced that this was all there was to life, she resigned herself to an existence of exhaustion and exclusion. Her bucket wasn't the only empty thing she lugged to the well every day.

When Jesus asked her for a drink, perhaps her first thought was, *Oh, great, another man, another favor.* I have to wonder, though, what happened between the woman and her God in the months and years before she met the Messiah. I can't accept that the intersection of their lives at Jacob's well was coincidence. I believe that moment was the answer to her prayers, the ones that seemed to ricochet off the ceiling, whether she knew it or not. God saw every tear she had cried privately, every drop of life that had flowed from her frustration, fatigue, and fear. Not one drop had left her eyes without the tender attention and compassion of her Maker, her true Husband.[9] I want to believe that she cried out to God as she continued singlehandedly to care for the daily needs of husband, hearth, and home. It seemed that as soon as she filled the bucket, it was drained, demanding another trek to the watering hole. So, once again, she came alone looking for replenishment. This day, she found the Lord and left with *living* water.

As I read that day, my thirsty soul swallowed hard. Living water is the missing ingredient in the world's recipe for resilience. All the CrossFit® workouts, low-carb diets, girls' nights out, creativity, and napping combined aren't capable of satisfying the scorched soul. Jesus said, "Everyone who drinks this water will get thirsty again and again. Anyone who drinks the water I give will never thirst—not ever. The water I give will be an artesian spring within, gushing fountains of endless life."[10]

As we continue to love and live with our warriors, the first and most important step toward preventing burnout is bringing our bucket to His well of living water and drawing deeply for that day's supply. The next time your circumstances demand another drink, remember "the gift of God and who it is who asks you for a drink." Ask Him for living water before you fill anyone else's bucket. Then you can confidently meet the need at hand from a place of abundance. At the same time, this living water will become in you "a spring of water welling up to eternal life."

God offers us living water, the only reliable reservoir of refreshment for the human heart. By faith, the source flows from Him through His Son, Jesus Christ, to us. His living water quenches our dusty lives and pours a sparkling spring into every nook and cranny of our heart. This living water is our best remedy for the compassion fatigue brought on by the hardships on our home front.

Questions for Reflection

1. How do you know when you are burned out? Describe yourself physically, mentally, and spiritually when you've reached the end of your rope.

2. Based on the causes of compassion fatigue found on pages 94–95, what do you think are the *three biggest reasons* for your own feelings of burn-out?

3. Have you taken any of the following steps to break the negative cycle of compassion fatigue in your life? If so, which steps have been most beneficial to you?

- Accept that the situation *itself* is stressful.

- Share your feelings with a trusted friend, co-worker, or trusted family member.

- Listen to others and acknowledge their perspective about the situation.

- Enhance your communication skills with your warrior and with your family.

- Improve your anger-management skills.

- Take positive action to change your daily environment.

- Exercise good time management. Learn how to distinguish between needs and wants.

- Commit to daily physical exercise.

- Commit to regular counseling and improving mental health.

- Commit to strengthening faith and improving spiritual health.

- Listen to your body and practice healthy self-care.

- Take time away from your stressful situation. Make a date with yourself weekly and replenish your mind and soul.

- Allow others to help you.

4. How has this changed your life for the better?

5. Let's go deeper:

All of us struggle at times with the inability to say no. This is referred to as a lack of personal boundaries. We learn what we have lived. Think about your family of origin. The ability to recognize our personal boundaries is a skill that is often modeled or taught during our formative years.

Looking back at your original family, were healthy life-coping skills modeled, such as healthy personal boundaries and proper self-care?

Share what you learned from your own parents/family of origin about coping with stress. (For example, how did your mother/father deal with anxiety, fears, and prolonged stressors? How did your older siblings handle these?) What patterns do you find in your coping skills that mirror these?

6. Do you have a favorite Bible verse that speaks to your heart about fatigue or renewal of strength? What is it?

6

It's His What It Is: Our New Normal

Being confident of this, that he who began a good work in you will carry it on to completion until the day of Christ Jesus.

Philippians 1:6

No matter how hard I searched, I couldn't find them. I had looked everywhere for weeks. I was exhausted and resigned myself to the sad fact that I'd probably never see them again. I missed my toes. The hard watermelon that hung low beneath my shirt was our first child, and he was due any moment.

It was mid-June in Phoenix. When I wasn't waddling around at work, I wallowed in the shallow end of my parents' pool. I displaced so much water that mathematically I couldn't sink. From my pinky toes to the tip of my nose, every cell in my body was about to burst.

My labor pains interrupted the 1986 nail-biting season finale of *Dynasty*. Mark and I headed for our Honda Prelude and sped into the unknowns of parenthood. My father followed us to the hospital while my mom stayed behind and prayed, translating her faith and fears into an all-night housecleaning vigil.

My copy of *What to Expect When You're Expecting* was dog-eared, stained, and torn. I had studied well for this final exam and was confident I would pass with flying colors. Mark and I rehearsed the breathing exercises we had learned at Lamaze classes as we turned into the parking lot. Back home, our baby's nursery was brimming with bright yellow blankets, lacy bunting, and tiny Pampers. Everything on the outside was in place, but nothing could have prepared me for what was about to happen to my mind, spirit, and body as a new and slippery soul emerged.

After seven hours of my screaming and pain, Joshua Carter Waddell slid onto this planet. Josh relaxed into the warmth of my chest and I fell in love with him. He was the most marvelous and miraculous mess I had ever made.

Change is always messy. It never arrives in a pristine package. Change is usually deposited on our doorstep in a tangled ball of knots that we must bravely tackle and patiently unravel.

The End of the World

Whether they recount the details of a natural disaster, a personal violation, or the experience and effects of war, every survivor of trauma will agree that the shock, the shattering, and the mess left in its wake constituted the end of their perfect life as they knew it.

I spent about two years trying to get things back to normal. We occasionally went out to dinner and used to spend several evenings during the week having quality time before PTSD was diagnosed. We had a good balance in our family. My husband became very detached and uninterested in being part of the family during his most difficult times in his battle with

PTSD. To counteract that, I began to designate our Friday nights as family nights so that it became more predictable and no excuses could be made not to be home. I began doing frequent purposeful planning to have things to look forward to so that life would be more predictable and positive.

While my warrior was in treatment we kept talking of things we would do and how it would be at home, etc. When he got home I kept trying to make these things we discussed a reality and make our lives back to the way it used to be, but nothing I did helped and rarely anything we discussed about how things would be was actually followed.

Though we all refused to acknowledge it for a time, though we were locked in an exhausting, messy tug-of-war between what was and what is, those of us who love and live with a combat veteran now must admit that the place we lived, the plans we had, and the paradise we knew predeployment are no longer on the map. Our loved ones' wartime experiences took their toll on our veteran, on us, and also on the terrain of our home front.

In your mind's eye, place a snapshot of your pre-war family or marriage beside a snapshot of your post-war family or marriage. Compare the two images for a moment. What differences do you see between the two images? Does your comparison resonate with the comparisons of other military family members?

In my snapshot of our pre-war marriage and young family things were so calm and still. It was bright and peaceful. Life moved a little smoother and it was easy. This family had big dreams. I looked so confident. My husband was tall and strong; he was fearless and trustworthy. Life seemed effortless. It was easy to look toward the future and both of us see the same goal. We walked together hand in hand, down the same road at the same speed to reach that goal. If one of us was tired, we could easily carry one another. In our post-war family, we look tired, aged, and lonely. We have to work a lot harder to move ahead in life.

Before, we were all laid back and relaxed. Life was happy and exciting. Now we are surrounded by an intensity that seems to almost always be lingering around us. We used to love being outside, but now we mainly stay inside and only talk about doing this or that. We used to be surrounded with friends, always trying to plan get-togethers, but that happens rarely now. There was a lot of laughter, a lot of joking around. Now we have to be careful because moods and tones interfere and prevent lightheartedness. Things are easily misinterpreted these days.

I stared at the pictures on my desk, one before he was wounded and one from this past summer. In the pre-war photo, my warrior and I are standing in front of our military base housing by our flag. He is in uniform. I was about twenty pounds heavier. Stress caused me to lose weight. We are both smiling and his arm is around my shoulder. My arms are wrapped around his waist and we are very close. We are happy to be in each others' arms. The smiles on our faces are carefree and genuine. My warrior has pride on his face. I was proud to be standing by my warrior. Our love is apparent on our faces and in our body language. We were oblivious to what lay ahead of us.

In the post-war photo, we are at my hometown by the lake for a family reunion. I am much smaller. I still haven't regained the weight. His military uniform, which will never be worn again, is now hanging in the closet. My warrior is by my side, but there is a gap between us, an invisible wall only we can see and feel. Our arms are not holding each other tight. My arm is around his waist, but his is just barely holding me.

His cane is in his other hand, stabilizing his stance. The day was warm but our smiles are not as warm. They are different, not as carefree as in the pre-war shot. The smiles hide trauma inside and out. My warrior's shorts reveal the scars on his legs from the many surgeries, but the scars on our hearts and minds are invisible to anyone besides us.

Here and Gone in a New York Minute

At the midpoint of Operation Iraqi Freedom, *Time* magazine featured an article titled "Looking for the New Baghdad." The article focused on how Iraq's capital had changed. It highlighted the progress, but was careful to underscore that "the gains that have been made are fragile."[1]

The writer used words throughout the text that are synonymous with fragile, such as *vulnerable* and *tenuous*. He weaved into the text phrases such as "something terrible is about to happen," "bracing for a turn for the worse," and "just like that, we can fall into hell again." I couldn't help but draw a parallel between Iraq's new normal and the new "normal" that is my marriage, family, and home front as a result of Iraq.

We can't keep defaulting to the ideas that worked before the war. The relational routes we knew by heart are now crisscrossed with new patterns that complicate communication. Our new normal is filled with tenuous starts and stops, but we must continue to ask for, allow for, and strive for a new pattern of daily living.

Back to Basics

When everything around us has changed, something within us must too. Changes of the heart are messy. Like the biblical Jonah, we need to come to the place where, even though we're covered in fish vomit, we are headed in the direction God intended for us all along. In what was the darkest week of my life, I was helped in the right direction by my Jewish neighbor, Lisa. When she rang the doorbell to deliver a hug, I invited her inside. Knowing my heart was fragile, she talked of other things besides the obvious. She and her family would be lighting the third candle of Hanukkah that night. She explained to me that Hanukkah was a holiday about rededication. I knew the story, but I listened to it again, wondering what Hanukkah had to do with my heartbreak.

Eight generations before Jesus was born, an evil Syrian general ransacked Jerusalem and desecrated its temple. Then he erected an altar to Zeus in the holy place and sacrificed a dirty pig on the altar. Everything in my living room faded to the periphery except my neighbor's face. She continued to talk, but I heard no words. She had just described the condition of the temple of my heart. The most sacred places in my life, my marriage and my family, had been ransacked and desecrated by the aftermath of war. My rebellious response to it all had made a huge mess of God's home, my heart. There I stood, speechless in my own hollowed-out holy of holies, trying to catch my breath, dwarfed by my own idolatries and standing in a puddle of vileness. Hanukkah had everything to do with my heartbreak. God was inviting me to a time of rededication to himself and the letting go of what was and would never be again, and a return to the basics. God had sent Lisa, a modern-day Maccabaeus, to my house to help me see my need.

I cried on and off for several days. No, I *wailed* with my forehead on the floor. Crying is messy business too. I make embarrassing choking and drowning sounds as the rivers of pain flow out. Times like these require large supplies of courage and tissues.

Although it was much harder to accept the first couple of years, it is getting easier. It is obviously disappointing that we will never be able to do a lot of the activities we once enjoyed, but we are at least trying, even though it doesn't yet feel comfortable most of the time.

I pray a lot. I try to make the time easier for him by stating exactly where we are going, what we will be doing, and how much time it will take. Then, if things don't go as quickly, I try to make light of the situation, a sort of distraction of time. I joke or try to engage him in a conversation he would find of great interest. I ask him questions which require more than a yes or no answer.

I know we are accepting our new normal when suggestions of trying new things or old things are not met with as much anger, frustration, or the need for isolation. He still chooses isolation over social situations, but we are working on that. We don't have many people left in our life. Some simply moved away thanks to the military, but most of them severed relationships because they don't know how to cope with us. I hope and pray God will bring new people into our world, but mostly that He will reunite our family ties that have been broken.

Talking through issues with our therapist has helped us accept our new normal. I also had to realize that no matter what I did or said, nothing could change things and no one could change the situation no matter how hard we might have tried on our own.

We have moved toward our new normal only with a lot of time and prayer and really giving it to God. I have learned to trust that this is His plan for us. I don't try to go back to the way things were. Instead, I work to try to make life as wonderful as possible with where we are now.

I received a birthday card from my in-laws. It read, "As we grow older, it's important to remember that life is all about how you handle Plan B."

I loved the card; but after a little more thought realized something important. God's Word tells me that there is no such thing as Plan B. Jeremiah 29:11 clarifies that this is still Plan A: "'For I know the plans I have for you,' declares the LORD, 'plans to prosper you and not to harm you, plans to give you hope and a future.'" This phenomenon that professionals call the New Normal is really just another page, another chapter in God's book about our days, which "were written . . . before one of them came to be."[2] The challenge for us, His children, who by nature default to hating life's messiness, is finding the miracle in the mess. Someone wisely said that without the mess there is no message. God is trusting us to find the treasures and the gifts in our days.

This doesn't mean that He wants us to walk around masking the pain with denial. We must face the facts and admit plainly what has been lost on our home fronts. However, we then need to work toward accepting His plan and His eternal perspective.

Acceptance is arriving at the place of true change, and true change is always messy. It's true. I lost the man I married. It's true, the family we built has been reframed. The one who deployed did not return home to us. We accept that loss and have begun to look for the gifts found only in grief.

Not every part of our lives was lost, though. For us, what endured are our common faith in Christ, our love for one another, and our hope in God's promises. Today we are learning how to rebuild our relationship from the foundation upward, to grow in affection and intimacy, and to laugh together again.

We will never be the same couple or family that we were before his combat deployments. Yet as we rebuild we are learning to work together in the wisdom and strength of God and to balance this labor of love with patience, times of rest and retreat.

Stated in a get-over-it, get-on-with-it tone of voice with a shrug of the shoulders, and followed by a heavy sigh, the phrase "It is what it is" has become our twenty-first century white-flag resignation when speaking of the lousy hand we've been dealt. Those within earshot nod in long-faced agreement. I propose a twist: It's *His* what it is. Instantly, my face isn't as long because of the reminder that God is in control. We can trust the gifts He gives us, even those that come wrapped in grief. "Every good and perfect gift is from above, coming down from the Father of the heavenly lights."[3] The good gifts are the ones we understand and appreciate right away. The *perfect* gifts are often the very things we fear, the things that are pregnant with life if we will only believe Him. And by His strength and steadfast love, I'm learning to trust Him when my life leaves the realm of the comfortable and controllable and leaps into seeming chaos. I'm slowly getting better at keeping my inner compass aligned with His Word as we navigate our new normal even when all roads and relationships are a mess.

I think about the day of the cross. Sweat turned to blood. Flesh hung in red ribbons. Blood and water sprayed. Then it happened. At three in the afternoon, Jesus of Nazareth slid off this planet. Christ's death, the biggest mess in history, made real change possible for me. Now I can relax into the warmth of His love. I have fallen in love with Him. I am grateful for Golgotha, the messiest delivery room ever.

Questions for Reflection

1. We hear the term *new normal* frequently. In the context of a wounded warrior's family experience, the new normal refers to the way life is *now* compared to the way life was *before* the combat deployment(s).

   Honestly, how do you feel when others refer to your challenges as your "new normal"?

2. In your mind's eye, place a snapshot of your pre-war family/marriage beside a snapshot of your post-war family/marriage. Compare the two images for a moment.

Now describe the differences you see in the two snapshots (facial expressions, body language, background or setting, lighting, sounds, colors, activity). Give as much detail as you can.

3. Was there a period of time that you tried to get things "back to normal"? If so, describe an example.

4. Have you accepted or begun to accept that the predeployment normal no longer exists for you and your family?

   If so, who or what helped you to do so?

   If so, how do you know you have accepted or are beginning to accept your new normal?

5. *"It is what it is."* How does this popular saying make you feel right now?

6. *"It's His what it is."* How does this twist on the popular saying make you feel?

7

New from the Inside Out

Breaking the Cycle of Compassion Fatigue

> May God himself, the God of peace, sanctify you
> through and through. May your whole spirit,
> soul and body be kept blameless at the coming
> of our Lord Jesus Christ. The one who calls you
> is faithful, and he will do it.
>
> 1 Thessalonians 5:23–24

Most of us don't own a comma bag. That's a new term I learned when I moved to Texas. I overheard a wealthy oil and gas man in Fort Worth say that he knows just what to do when he and his wife are at odds. He buys her a comma bag, a purse that has a price with a comma in it, and all is well again. The two most outrageous comma bags I've heard about are the Louis Vuitton Tribute Patchwork handbag, priced at $45,000, and the diamond-encrusted Hermes Crocodile Birkin, priced between

$80,000 to $130,000, depending on how much bling you want. I never knew that the combination of purses and price tags with the right punctuation had the power to make problems disappear!

Naturally I was curious when I opened the invitation to a friend's handbag party: "45 Purses in One!" I'm not typically a Tupperware or Silpada Designs jewelry party kind of girl, but the thought of getting forty-five different purses in one intrigued me. The hostess welcomed us to her home, and after some light appetizers and conversation, the purse representative gave her pitch. The concept was clever. All I had to do was purchase the basic black bag and an outer shell or two (or ten). The brightly colored and textured purse shells were magnetic and fit snugly around the basic black bag. This meant that I would never again have to empty, sort out, or reorganize the contents of my purse to be admirably accessorized. I would only have to slap on a different magnetic shell to match that day's outfit or mood as I headed out the door. Genius! And the price tag had no commas.

I took the bait and bought the set, one basic bag and three shells, and embarked on a new lifestyle of sneaky shortcuts toward fashion sophistication. I welcomed anything that could simplify my scattered life. Even though life on the home front was chaotic, at least I could be color coordinated.

For a while, I enjoyed my newfound smart fashion solution. Before sprinting out the back door every morning, I selected and slapped a snazzy shell around my basic black bag. I'd sling the bag over my right shoulder and start my day with a flare of fashion-induced confidence. At first this little ritual only required a few seconds of my time. After a few weeks, though, I had to spend a few extra minutes stuffing the basic bag, now a bit bulkier, into its shell. This daily exercise demanded more and more of my once-streamlined mornings as my basic black bag began to bulge with all the stuff I continued to collect and carry around. My daughters began to refer to my purse as my other child because it scored its own seat in restaurants and rode shotgun in the car. A few folks even asked where I was traveling with that carry-on.

My neck began to ache. I noticed I had started leaning to the left in order to balance the weight on my right and still achieve any forward motion. The morning I slung the bag over my right shoulder and suddenly found myself flailing around in an unattractive 360–degree spin was the day I reassessed my accessory.

The purse wasn't at fault, I concluded. I was. I was needlessly carrying around too much baggage. *How had my purse gotten so heavy?* I wondered. I was almost afraid to look. The luxury of never having to empty, sort out, or reorganize the growing contents of my purse, which had been the selling point for me at the party, had come with a hidden price tag. There was only one solution: take off the shell, empty the bag, sort out the contents, and start over.

My handbag held a meaningful metaphor for me: I couldn't keep slapping on a bright exterior over my inner emotional baggage either. The weight of my husband's combat stress, PTSD, and TBI had thrown my life off balance. My body and soul ached under the weight of our challenges on the home front. Yet I kept adopting a crowd-pleasing shell. I longed to be new from the inside out. There was only one solution: remove the masks, clear out the inner recesses of my heart, soul, mind, and body, sort and prioritize what absolutely must remain, and then start afresh.

In chapter six, we talked about letting go of what was. There are steps we as family members of warriors can take to strengthen ourselves while the personal and relational battles rage. God has provided much wisdom and sound counsel from reliable medical and mental health professionals and faith leaders that help us to better understand the responsibility that we each have. Our loving God wants us to be whole and effective. He has entrusted us with our minds, our bodies, and our souls. We have a role in caring for ourselves and fortifying ourselves. We don't want to merely weather this storm; we want to navigate it well.

Military life, and certainly military life with invisible wounds on the home front, demands daily resilience. I had to learn, mostly by trial and error, what makes a person resilient. Resilience is the ability to recoil or spring back into shape after bending or stretching. Think yoga pants and leggings. Resilience is the ability to withstand or to recover quickly from difficult conditions. It is the ability to recover from, to adapt, or to adjust to change. Think Gummi Bears. My teens entertained themselves one day for hours by placing several Gummi Bears behind our car tire, then backing up over them, putting the car in drive and rolling over them a second time, sometimes three and four times. I could hear their laughter and amazement as the Gummi Bears always sprang back to their original shape. I want to be like the Gummis. I want to be practically indestructible in an adorable kind of way. They must have a secret ingredient that keeps them tough and together. They have much in common with family members of combat veterans who have learned the secrets to resilience.

Creating a Recipe for Resilience

The recipe that I have found to work well in a home and family dealing with compassion fatigue has only five ingredients. I was inspired by Shannon Wexelberg's song "Cling,"[1] and found that using it as an acrostic, CLING, helps me remember the recipe. These are the five steps I took and still take to create an environment of healing for myself.

C—*Connect* **with your Creator, your close friends, your community ministries, and your counselor.** I went to God. More frequently on my face than on my knees, I called on the Lord. I set aside time that I could be alone daily in His presence. Sometimes I sprinted into His throne room. Other days I could barely crawl to the edge of His courtyards. Either way Jesus met me at my point of need and walked with me into the presence of our Father. I relied on my Savior to intercede for me and on His Holy Spirit to pray for me when I couldn't find the words. While my human tendency in my pain was to pull away from God and from other believers, I made the commitment to guard my one-on-one times with God and to continue to worship and fellowship with His family—come what may.

We need to connect with God first and then to make every effort to connect to those who strengthen and support us. I'm talking about the support we find in competent physicians, mental health care professionals, experienced counselors, pastors, helpful books, and solid organizations.

I prayerfully sought godly female professional help. At that time my warrior wouldn't agree to counseling. I chose to pursue help regardless. I went to my counselor regularly for more than two years before we had to move again. This step was a healing balm to my wounds. I've been told that most veterans who have sought mental health care and counseling say they did so because his or her spouse patiently led the way.

The strength I found by connecting with God and with an experienced counselor enabled me to reach out and to connect with others on this journey. Living with the invisible wounds of war is impossible to do single-handedly. We need to be like Navy SEALs and build a winning team. They believe that two are better than one and a team is even better. The smallest units in SEAL training and operations are pairs—sniper pairs, SCUBA pairs, swimming pairs, scout pairs. "Swim buddies" know one another's strengths and weaknesses.

SEALs also know the importance of mentors—seasoned, respected SEALs they refer to as "sea daddies." Companionship, accountability, and team building are critical ingredients in a recipe for resilience. Our equivalent of the SEALs' swim buddies and sea daddies are the men and women we can build into our team as priceless resources of information, guidance, and compassion.

Who's on your personal team? Who can you identify that you believe can contribute to your health, balance, and wellness? Who are the people and the organizations you can build into your support system?

L—*Learn* **all you can as you lean into the Lord.** Weekly Christian counseling gave me the motivation and the strength to educate myself about PTSD and TBI. I read everything I can get my hands on, being careful to look at all of it through the lens of scriptural principles. My research gives me the information and perspective I need to better understand my warrior's pain, its source, its logic, and its potential. Please refer to the recommended reading list and other resources listed in Appendix C of this book.

I—*Intercede* **for others—and get intercession.** I called in reinforcements. I put my best prayer warriors on active duty. I asked my closest, most trusted sisters in Christ to pray for us without ceasing. The enemy's plan is so simple: to separate believers, isolate them, and squelch their ability to glorify God.

Who are the potential spiritual reinforcements you can call onto active duty on your behalf? Find two or three individuals whose faith in God and in His Son is mature, consistent, and proven genuine by their character. Ask these individuals to intercede for you and your family, to provide the prayer coverage you and your family need in the special circumstances of post-war stress. Keep them updated weekly in a brief phone call or email. When tensions spike or crises erupt at home, let them know that you need immediate prayer.

N—*Nourish* **your body, mind, and spirit.** Vitality and personal wholeness require doing something daily that strengthens your physical body, your mind, and your spirit.

Take your physical temperature. Are you staying active? Start taking care of yourself today. Start with small steps, something as simple as stopping your nail-biting habit. Pay attention to your body. Are you chewing the inside of your cheek, rubbing your eyebrows off, or pulling on your eyelashes unconsciously? Are your shoulders up in your ears due to the tension in your neck? Are you remembering to take cleansing breaths or are you barely breathing?

Then take a look at some of the bigger health issues—smoking cessation, paying attention to and getting help for eating disorders such as bulimia or binging, and making a commitment to improve your daily diet to include more fresh vegetables and fruits and fewer alcoholic and soft drinks. These decisions are not easy to make alone. Enlist an accountability partner or support group as you make these lifestyle adjustments.

There is a difference between being physically active and being in a constant state of random movement and busyness. Love yourself enough to take care of the body you live in and depend on every day. An effective physical exercise plan doesn't have to cost an arm and a leg. Any number of "get healthy" websites have free downloadable articles, workout videos, and suggested exercises for targeting specific muscle groups. You'll find guidance for safe weight loss, for preventing heart disease, cancer, and depression, and for managing fibromyalgia and other chronic pain issues.

According to Lt. Col. Dave Grossman, author of *On Combat: The Psychology and Physiology of Deadly Conflict in War and in Peace*, "Sleep deprivation is a key factor in PTSD and malnourishment and suicides. The stressors amplify one another. The surest way to inflict wounds on loved ones or yourself is to operate from sleep deprivation. The best way you can prevent further wounding is to avoid sleep deprivation. Sleep is a biological blind spot for us. Sleep deprivation is a weak link in our pursuit of health. Establish your own curfew. Make rest a priority because you love others and yourself."[2]

If the truth be known, maybe you're struggling right now as you read this chapter on the importance of taking care of yourself. You are struggling to keep your eyes open, struggling to stay focused, wrestling with all the voices in your head reminding you of all the things you simply *must* do today while you sleepily dream of a caffeine-loaded drink. Am I right?

You've lived in overdrive so long that it has become the norm. You've forgotten how it is to feel any different. But don't worry. You're not alone. We refuel our cars, recharge our cell phones, recycle our trash, restock our refrigerators, and even insist that our babies have their naps. Yet we don't do the same for *ourselves*. We simply don't know when enough is enough. We don't know how to stop and relax anymore.

That's not God's design or desire for us. God's order of things is in perfect balance. Day and night. Summer and winter. Fall and spring. Planting and harvest. Hot and cold. Light and dark. God has designed His creation, which includes us, with the need and the opportunity for rest. He not only *made* His creation with this in mind, but He has *mandated* periods of rest. Nonstop work, the absence of refreshment and rest, and an epidemic of chronic fatigue are no laughing matter. In fact, that kind of life is not what God intended for us. Further, God has created and commanded something much different from the pace that we insist on keeping.[3]

There is a reason God gave us the fourth commandment, when He told us not to do any work one day a week.[4] He gave us the seventh day of the week as a gift, one full twenty-four-hour cycle simply to stop. He gave us permission to be still, to reflect, to slow down . . . guilt-free. Spend some down time exploring the life-changing concept of biblical Sabbath. Need a nap? Take it! Carve out time to come away and rest awhile.

There is a time to work. There is a time to rest. And there is resting while working. Jesus said that He is the true Vine and that we, His followers, are the branches. He reminds us that a branch separated from the energy and life of the vine can do absolutely nothing. He gives us one item for our to-do list: stay connected to the Vine. As children of God and believers in Jesus Christ, our one aim each day is to remain in the Vine, to remain in Jesus every hour, every minute. In this way, we will learn from Him what true rest is and experience that true rest even in the whirlwind of our demanding lives.[5]

Take your mental temperature. Are you feeding your mind? Are you learning something new? Do you have an outlet of creative expression, such as journaling, painting, theater, or music?

This morning the silence ends. I need to write. I don't have a plan or a theme. I only know I must pull this pen across the page and allow my spirit to speak through the ribbons of ink I am tying across it. I look for love. I look for truth. My pen is the light with which I search. I look. I listen. I see. I hear. I know.

The most helpful thing I did was to lose weight. Last year I lost twenty-eight pounds. This year my goal is to lose twenty-five more.

Running usually clears my head and helps me to regain perspective. Some people are able to pray when they exercise, but I can't. I exercise to mentally clear the static and to calm my soul. Then I feel much more prepared to handle whatever is coming my way.

I remember consciously giving myself permission to take care of me. I committed to physical exercise several times a week, made time for fun with my girlfriends, and made (and kept) appointments for my own medical and dental exams. I learned a new craft by signing up for a class and made new friends in the process. The first step, though, was giving myself permission to love myself to the same extent that I loved my warrior and my family.

Take your spiritual temperature. I get my favorite soul food fix from Mama Dip's, an unassuming house-turned-restaurant on a quiet corner in Carrboro, North Carolina. I head there every chance I can to get a taste of home. There are times in my life when only stewed okra and tomatoes, black-eyed peas, collard greens with vinegar, salt-cured country ham, a sweet-potato biscuit, and sweet tea will do. I put that first bite in my mouth, close my eyes, and I am instantly transported back in time to my grandmother's kitchen, a place I loved to be, a place I called home.

Just as our bodies and our emotional ties to our homeland crave a taste of home, so do our spirits. Our souls crave a taste of our true home, heaven, where God is enthroned. This taste of home is found by spending time in His Word, in fellowship with other believers, in awe of an aspect of His creation, and in individual and corporate worship.

You have Someone greater and bigger than you, past what you can see, who lives and works in the unseen realm. You have a Father-child relationship with the One who has all the details of your life—past, present, and future—sorted out. Do you know His personality, His character, and His promises to you? Do you know that He loves you intensely, unconditionally, and perfectly, just as you are, right where you are? Plug into a fellowship of like-minded believers and feed your faith daily through quiet personal meditation and Bible study.[6]

Putting the Lord and Bible time first helps my day to go better. I make a point to be in a Bible study, to spend time in prayer, and to read encouraging books. This helps me to focus on the truth and I am less likely to slip into depression and withdrawal.

Sometimes I go to the park and walk with a note card or pad of paper and pen. I talk with God and give Him all of my worries.

I have found comfort in the psalms. For the first time, I feel I truly have a kinship with the psalmist, who wrote about

*darkness and desolation. My times are in God's hands. I have
to give my circumstances to Him daily and ask for strength
for that day's demands.*

*The Word of God was alive and active to me even in the
middle of sleepless nights. I always could go back to sleep
once I had talked with the Lord about what was troubling me.*

G—*Give* **back; get involved.** "Do not neglect your gift, which
was given you through prophecy when the body of elders laid their
hands on you. Be diligent in these matters; give yourself wholly
to them, so that everyone may see your progress. Watch your life
and doctrine closely. Persevere in them, because if you do, you
will save both yourself and your hearers" (1 Timothy 4:14–16).
You and I have each been uniquely gifted to serve others. A time
will come when your emotions are not as raw, a time when the
pieces of your story will start to come together, a time when you
may sense a desire to invest what you've learned along the way
into the lives of others. The pain and suffering that God allows
to take place in our lives is not without purpose. Though it is difficult to see when we are hurting, God has others in mind, others
who need our wisdom, our strength, and the inspiration of our
courage down the road.

When invited to share the story of our family's experience with
PTSD publicly for the first time in 2007, I was afraid, but I did it.
This led to other opportunities and later to an invitation to be on
the writing team for the *When War Comes Home* manual. And
God has not only given you a story that needs to be told, but a
unique set of skills to creatively tell your story.

*It has helped me to speak out on behalf of others who are
suffering, led by the Holy Spirit, reaching out to family members in similar situations. I advocate and educate wherever
God gives me the opportunity.*

I refused to let my warrior become a recluse. It's a lot of work to be hospitable to family and friends, but it pays big dividends. We invite family and friends into our home. I make it happen.

I am trying to stay in touch with others who have been through what we are going through. I started a support group for families of veterans who have PTSD. My group helps me to feel not so alone, isolated, and misunderstood. It helps a lot to have the company of people who understand.

We are told in 2 Corinthians 1:3–4 to comfort others with the comfort we ourselves have received from God. Ask God how and when He would have you to give back, how He would have you to serve others using the skill set and the unique strengths He entrusted to you. You will begin to find a greater healing than you ever thought possible. By giving back, by getting involved, by paying it forward, you will find a greater measure of freedom and joy.

Now is the time to stop slapping new covers over the inner you. No matter how many compliments you receive about how well others think you are holding it all together, you and I know there are times when the baggage simply gets too heavy to lug around any longer. Look at all that you have collected and continue to carry around needlessly. We encourage you to dump the contents of your mind, body, and spirit onto God's kitchen counter, sort it out with His help, and start over.

The cover concept works in the handbag world; applying this approach to the way we care for ourselves is not a good idea. Through His Son, Jesus, God has provided the way for us to be new from the inside out. He never slaps a new magnetic cover over the inner person. His Word says, "Therefore, if anyone is in Christ, he is a new creation; the old has gone, the new has come."[7] God has entrusted us with a conscious mind that has the ability to think, reason, and feel emotions, an eternal spirit made in His image with which we communicate with Him, and a physical body to cart the other two around. He expects us to nurture all three in order to have the endurance, the wisdom, and the faith required to win the battles on the home front.

Questions for Reflection

1. Describe how you recognize mental fatigue in yourself.

2. What do you find to be most helpful in coping with it?

3. Describe how you recognize physical fatigue in yourself.

4. What do you find to be most helpful in coping with it?

5. Describe how you recognize spiritual fatigue in yourself.

6. What do you find to be most helpful in coping with it?

8

Faithful Body Parts
and the Power of Friendship

> Two are better than one, because they have a
> good return for their work: If one falls down,
> his friend can help him up. But pity the man who
> falls and has no one to help him up!
>
> Ecclesiastes 4:9–10 (NIV 1984)

I'm having a hysterectomy in a month, and decided to throw a party.

I've selected an appropriate date. My celebration will take place on the next full moon. This is in honor of all womankind whose whims, wombs, and waistlines wax full and wane thin on a lunar cycle. My guest list includes every female friend and family member I have. No boys allowed.

I realize I strayed from the path of traditional party themes. I am trusting that a generous amount of humor added to an asymmetrical party plan along with the support of my closest girlfriends

131

will carry me through the highs and lows of the emotional roller coaster of a hysterectomy. Family and friends gladly gather to celebrate *life* cycles, such as birthdays, anniversaries, and graduations. Why not celebrate this cycle too, with great flare and appreciation for a faithful body part?

A good sense of humor and the support of my most trusted girlfriends are a winning combination for facing the bigger challenges I encounter in life. This is especially true as I figure out how to manage the invisible wounds of war on the home front.

The Flavors and Faces of Friendship

As adults, our days include co-workers and assorted allies with whom we share a common cause (sometimes translated a common enemy). There are social friends, those who come into our lives because they like to scrapbook or study wise investing or do yoga or Zumba like we do. We have new friends, good friends, longtime friends, former friends, remembered friends, and the crown jewel, the maraschino on the sundae of sisterhood, our best friend.

With all these flavors of friends to fill the human-shaped gaps and spaces in our lives, why do we feel so desperately alone in life's darkest places? Part of the answer to that question is our choice, whether it's conscious or not, to retreat into ourselves. When a stressful situation is prolonged, such as the effects of PTSD and TBI on the home front, our natural tendency is to withdraw from important friendships and healthy interactive activities. We isolate ourselves and drop off the radar in an attempt to survive the storm, just when the need for friends is the most urgent.

I was very embarrassed about what we were going through. I also did not want to blemish my husband's reputation. I knew that I could forgive my husband for the things that he was doing, but I also knew that my friends and family were going to have a more difficult time forgiving the things he was doing to our family.

It is impossible to tiptoe around your wounded warrior, day in and day out, while taking care of all of life's other duties (duties that normally are shared between two people). I felt overly angry, depressed, exhausted, overwhelmed, and just wanted to be alone.

I pulled away from the activities that simply required too much time or effort; I had to prioritize which activities and friends were helpful and healthy during the most difficult times. I had to take care of myself.

At the beginning, I was so busy taking care of my warrior, house, kids, finances, etc., that I just didn't have time for friends. I quit doing just about everything I used to do.

When War Comes Home, *Don't* Retreat

I won't let you do this.

A bold text message from a new friend instantly challenged my own withdrawal from friends a few years ago. I had hit the ignore button on my phone one too many times. Cassie refused to give up. By text, she let me know she was concerned for me, and would not allow me to cut myself off from my friends. She understood enough about my heartaches to know that isolating myself would only make matters worse. Only a woman who's been there, done that, learns to speak boldly. Cassie would not allow the ones she loved to isolate to their own destruction.

War had come home. With Cassie's and others' encouragement, I decided I wouldn't retreat. When I asked for and received the prayers of my best friends, I set aside the heavy stigma a diagnosis of PTSD brings with it and became purposely outspoken about our experiences at home. I recognized I had to emerge from isolation and find a sisterhood—older women, younger women, and those my age—who were traveling through the same dark place. I chose to believe that the bonds of womanhood would bring a large measure of healing to my wounds.

Soul-level sadness is the final stop in the process of grief before healing can begin. The effect that PTSD and TBI has on the warrior's home has the quality of Gethsemane, a shadowy place where personal plans and dreams die an agonizing death. Although the Savior did it solo, God desires that His daughters be surrounded by an empathetic sisterhood of strength in their darkest hours of grief and loss. Military wives, mothers, daughters, and family members are typically self-sufficient.

As we stated in chapter three, family members of warriors are not "in the club," but that doesn't mean we are left alone. We are members of a very special and sizeable sisterhood of women who get it. You are not alone. Your love for your veteran and the hardships, adjustments, and sacrifices you've made connect you with every military family member in the history of mankind who found herself swept into the turbulent wake of war.

Kindred Spirits: A Word to My Sisters on the Home Front

According to iCasualties.org, the number of wounded warriors from both Operation Iraqi Freedom and Operation Enduring Freedom, as of November, 2012, was 50,212 wounded. Nearly every one of these warriors has parents. Half of them are married. The injuries of each wounded warrior affect at least ten family members and close friends. That means that there are at least half a million family members and close friends of warriors with *visible* wounds from Operation Iraqi Freedom and Operation Enduring Freedom alone. Add the warriors with *invisible* wounds to the mix and the sisterhood mushrooms to tens of millions of us.

We are family. We are related by blood, sweat of our stories is unique, and yet, each of our sto. We are bound together by the blood that our lov on foreign soil, the disfiguring burns, the broken limbs, and the deep bruises that took place on the ⌐₋ıι ıınes in service to our homeland.

We are related by the hard work, the diligence, the tenacity of standing by the one we love, and by staying strong for our children and grandchildren through good times and in difficult times. We are related by the challenge and hard work of finding and providing the care that our wounded warriors need 24/7, 365 days a year, both physically and psychologically.

We are related by the tears we cried the day we were told our loved one was to be deployed to war and again the day he or she left home. We are related by the tears we cried as we lay solo in a double bed night after night and by the tears we shed as we watched a generation of military kids grow up without their father or their mother around. We are related by the tears we shed the minute we learned that our loved one was injured, either visibly or invisibly, and by the tears we cry out of sheer exhaustion from shouldering the weight of meeting the demands of each day as we serve in yet another role, that of caregiver to the one we love. We are related by the tears we have all cried over our own wounds, the emotional and spiritual scars that no one can see, the invisible wounds of war that we ourselves carry around as loved ones of wounded warriors.

We are related to one another and we *need* one another. We need conversation and interaction with other women who are connected to the life and service of a combat veteran. It doesn't matter which wave of war caught us. Our common experiences transcend all generational and cultural boundaries. We need others who get it. We also need civilian friends, those who haven't necessarily walked a mile in our shoes, but sincerely want to understand our challenges and to lend practical support.

Your list of compassionate allies might be short, but a few true friends can make all the difference.

Staged to Sell: How We Appraise Others

I began packing up several areas of our home in Colorado last spring in preparation to move to Texas. Professional stagers coached me and told me that no potential homebuyer would want to see my family portraits, my clutter, my knickknacks, or any reference to time. So I dutifully wrapped, packed, and removed about 25 percent of our furniture and *schtuff* to "create space." The space was already there. It was just sprinkled, even blanketed with the business of living in that space, which I was told hinders the sale of a house. We are drawn to homes that are sterilized and staged. We offer higher selling prices and give them more value because they convince us that everything is in order, everything is clean, attractive, planned, comfortable, and pleasing to the eye. Therefore, the spaces where we lived couldn't look lived-in, only *semi* lived-in, model like, sterile, well—staged, but not stiff.

We prefer staged people, too, those people who seem to have all in order, thoughtfully planned and positioned, attractive physically and emotionally, clear of clutter and the issues of life, smiling, comfortable but swept clean and sparkling. We tend to lowball the people who seem cluttered, who are tripping over their well-lived-in spaces. We don't spend much time with the people who tend to get personal quickly, whose baggage and belongings weigh down the room.

I have never enjoyed or liked cover-ups. I have always asked the hard questions of others and given the hard answers when asked. I have experienced so many anonymous notes, whispered words of thanks, hugs and tears from other women who are thankful that I am willing to be honest. None of us face anything unique; there is not one person who has not experienced some sort of devastation in their life! The question is how we cope and move out of it.

What you see is what you get. I have no hidden agendas and I don't have time for folks who use them. My honesty challenges Christian women because so many of them live behind a façade. As a result the women who are suffering and feel marginalized by the rank and order find relief and healing within our classroom. Therefore, we clearly see that we are not alone and count ourselves blessed as sister warriors.

Too many of us on the home front are staged. We are worn out from trying to keep the clutter out and the counters cleared of all evidence of the toll war has taken on our families and relationships. We have no real friends because we ourselves are not authentic. We have become experts at avoiding the real issues and quickly lobbing a diversion for our easily distracted "friends." That's the profitable premise behind Facebook and other social media sites online. Facebook gives us instantaneous global connection to 600 million staged and sterile "friends" whom we "like," tag, post, poke, and comment about, but never really know. My pithy status might make you smile or wince or sigh.

I believe what's more important is what Facebook *doesn't* tell about me. It doesn't reveal what is really on my mind, who has "unfriended" me lately, what my family members honestly think about being related to me and vice versa, which friend of the hundreds listed in the sidebar are my true friends, which are merely creepers, or what was in the messages I never sent. Only God knows these things and maybe one or two girlfriends.

I pulled away from those individuals who did not, could not, or would not give me the support I needed at the time or whose own emotional disposition was lethal to my own

> *mental and emotional health. I liken it to cleaning out one's*
> *Facebook friends, identifying friends versus acquaintances,*
> *and identifying those with whom you want to truly share*
> *your personal business.*

I don't want to be defined by a pithy status. Nor do I want to be sterilized and staged, even if that connotes a higher value or commands more impressive selling points. I want the freedom and the space to be me.

Authenticity is the first quality I look for in a friend. Then I look for flexibility and optimism.

As I prepared to write today I talked with a very good friend of mine.

He is a combat veteran who did back-to-back deployments for sixteen years. He talks openly with me about his struggles. He unashamedly claims that it has been his faith in God that has enabled him to find hope and healing and solutions to the cries of his heart. Perhaps you've met him too. His name is David. King David. He is my wounded warrior friend.

> When the men were returning home [from war], the women came
> out from all the towns of Israel to meet King Saul with singing
> and dancing. . . . As they danced, they sang: "Saul has slain his
> thousands, and David his tens of thousands." (1 Samuel 18:6–7)

David is the best example of a combat trauma sufferer in the Bible. About three thousand years ago he uncovered his heart in the book of Psalms.

Because of David's songwriting, we know that he wrestled with combat stress. He wrestled with sleeplessness, nightmares, guilt, and an aching body. He cried himself to sleep. He knew the sting of betrayal by a trusted friend. He witnessed thousands falling at his side. He endured back-to-back deployments. He was guilty of fragging by his own orders and infidelity with a subordinate officer's wife. He experienced both defeat and victory in battle.

David gave us a timeless framework in Psalm 23 for answering a pressing question today: What do families affected by combat stress and the invisible wounds of war need? Allow me to go verse by verse to give you some ideas of what you can do to make a positive difference.

> The LORD is my shepherd, I shall not be in want.
> > He makes me lie down in green pastures,
> he leads me beside quiet waters,
> > he restores my soul.
> He guides me in paths of righteousness
> > for his name's sake.
> Even though I walk
> > through the valley of the shadow of death,
> I will fear no evil,
> > for you are with me;
> your rod and your staff,
> > they comfort me.
> You prepare a table before me
> > in the presence of my enemies.
> You anoint my head with oil;
> > my cup overflows.
> Surely goodness and love will follow me
> > all the days of my life,
> and I will dwell in the house of the LORD
> > forever. (NIV 1984)

> The LORD is my shepherd, I shall not be in want.

God is the Shepherd. God is the Healer. We aren't. Our job is to follow.

> He makes me lie down in green pastures,
> > he leads me beside quiet waters,

We need rest and quiet and a safe place to recover. We need healing, Sabbath, and for others to stop talking and listen. Those who are moving through the dark valley need the opportunity to tell their stories, uninterrupted and to interested persons. Talk. Find people who will let you talk. Find people who can keep it all confidential, and don't ask your warrior questions like "Did you kill anyone?" or "What did you see?" or "Why did you enlist?"

Storytelling requires an emotionally safe place, a trustworthy friendship. Yet many vets and their family members also need a safe place from physical harm. It is common for vets with PTSD to have self-destructive thoughts and/or suicidal thoughts. Some family members of veterans do too. Find friends who will offer their home as a refuge from the storm if that is ever needed.

> he restores my soul.
> He guides me in paths of righteousness
> for his name's sake.

Vets and those who live with them need a compass, a plan toward wholeness. That plan will include guidance to inspirational and informational resources, referrals to support groups or others in same boat, referrals to professionals including pastors/rabbis/spiritual leaders, medical professionals, and agency contacts.

> Even though I walk
> through the valley of the shadow of death,
> I will fear no evil,
> for you are with me;
> your rod and your staff,
> they comfort me.

We need others to walk *alongside* us through the dark stretch of life.

There are two types of PTSD sufferers: those who see PTSD as their new home, who have no intention of getting well or moving on, and those who are committed to passing through, who desire to get well and are teachable. The lie is that a vet and his/her family will never get out of this darkness, that his/her new, permanent address is in the valley of the shadow of PTSD. God tells us the opposite. His Word says we are traveling *through* it, not building our houses there. Veterans, spouses, and children need reminders that they are passing through this.[1]

> You prepare a table before me
> in the presence of my enemies.

Veterans and their families enjoy a basic home-cooked meal. Look for and accept your friends' old-fashioned hospitality. When you are invited to their home, go. Replenish your physical strength. Figuratively, David means that we need preachers, teachers, and ministers to teach and preach with excellence. Find nourishment with meat from the Word of God. Consider starting small support groups using *Hope for the Home Front* books and Bible studies and *When War Comes Home* workbooks and the *Combat Trauma Healing Manual* or other reliable resources by other authors, such as Sara Horn, Penny Monetti, Bea Fishback, and Jocelyn Green.

> You anoint my head with oil;

Veterans need prayer support, and so do you and your children. Let others know what you need in the way of prayer. Write your needs down so they can reread them. Many, many days are so dark that finding the words or energy to pray feels impossible, so ask for those who pray regularly to pray specifically for the needs of your military family.

> Surely goodness and love will follow me
> all the days of my life,
> and I will dwell in the house of the LORD
> forever.

Veterans and their families struggle with feelings of rootlessness and homelessness. "Where are you from?" is a difficult question to answer. We need reminders that God's presence is our home, here and for eternity, wherever we are stationed or posted or sent. We need reminders that we are "rooted and established" in His love for us[2] and that no government orders can change that.

Faithful Body Parts

God has been faithful to provide brothers and sisters for us along the military life journey. He gives that "grace to help us in our time of need"[3] by providing a "family" for me everywhere we have lived. He has kept His promise to "set the lonely in families."[4] Mothers, fathers, brothers, and sisters in the faith have always been miraculously and beautifully interwoven into the fabric of my life, each a strong cord that brings vivid color to God's design.

In Rhode Island, He sent Lynda, a sister in Christ, to be warm company during March snowstorms. He sent a sister, Gerrie, to welcome me to a new neighborhood in Hawaii, to laugh, to cry, to pray with me, and to yell and scream with me in the delivery room during my daughter's painful birth. He placed two sisters, Sherree and Melody, next door and around the corner, to listen to me, to understand me, and to love and help me to care for my children. He brought Jenny, who disliked shallow conversations about drapes and diapers but preferred soul-probing subjects that challenged my mind and fed my heart, discussed over zucchini bread and herbal tea. He encircled me with a group of ladies, spiritual cousins, who encouraged me and lifted me up in prayer every week. In Virginia, He even provided Nonie, a next-door surrogate grandmother, to school me in the Southern traditions of baking, canning, and gardening, to lavish my children with grandma hugs and attention, and to deliver soup, saltines, and 7-Up each time one of us looked peaked.

In Panama, He gave me another sister, Julia, to crack up with, to encourage me in the three-ring circus called homeschooling, and to be my sidekick in the *fruterías*, the fresh-produce markets downtown, in search of sugar cane and hot peppers. In Germany, God sent many precious women of faith into my life who became soul mates whom I'll love forever and prayer partners I know I can call on anywhere, anytime, for as long as I live.

Though my earthly family is priceless to me, I now realize that it is temporal. Only God's family is my true and lasting family. Jesus said, "'Who is my mother, and who are my brothers?' Pointing to his disciples, he said, 'Here are my mother and my brothers. For whoever does the will of my Father in heaven is my brother and sister and mother.'"[5]

Initially God sent mature Christian women into my life to intensely pray for me, my husband, and my two oldest children during a time when I simply needed to be held, cried with, and prayed for. He sent them to say the words I was simply too exhausted spiritually and emotionally to pray. God also provided an extremely spiritual and passionate priest who prayed warfare prayers for us and in our home.

It took so long for me to realize that I am not alone. I had read countless books, talked to doctors, etc. I knew there were others, but really did think our situation was unique. I wanted to know where everyone was. I wanted to know where the support groups were. I wanted to know why my warrior did not want to get help with me.

I always knew that war was not new. Wounded soldiers were not new. Families falling apart are not new. Nothing was new, but I just wanted to connect with just one person who got it. I tried to get a group going on our post for more than six months. I then began college and work, and then I gave up.

It wasn't until I attended the When War Comes Home Don't Retreat at Glen Eyrie Conference Center that I really felt no longer alone. I had now met others who get it. Realizing I am not alone was a huge turning point for me, a relief in a strange way. I had been convinced for so long that I was alone, even though I knew others were out there. I just didn't know how to find them. Now here I was in the presence of women who understood when I explained our life. I knew they got it. They had similar stories. Some stories were even much worse than mine. God bless them, God bless us all. I was amazed and deeply saddened at the same time.

We are all struggling through our own individual battles in our marriages, families, and friends. Our lives are forever changed.

I love my two best friends. They are supportive and so kind-hearted. God brought them both into my life for a reason and I am so thankful. I am still looking for new friends. I hope that through this support group I will find one or two. I need more friends who get it. I pray God will bring me new friends nearby so I can socialize more. I miss having more friends.

A Better PTSD

Jesus has called us His friends, and we could not ask for a truer friend than He. He demonstrated the purest form of friendship when He endured the punishment we deserve and died on the cross in our place. In John 15:12–15, He said, "This is My commandment, that you love one another as I have loved you. Greater love has no one than this, than to lay down one's life for his friends. You are My friends if you do whatever I command you. No longer do I call you servants, for a servant does not know what his master is doing; but I have called you friends, for all things that I heard from my Father I have made known to you." (NKJV)

As friends of Christ, we have been entrusted with a better PTSD:

P . . . You and I have the privilege to speak the promises of God into the lives of veterans and their families.

T . . . God has put His trust in you and me. He trusts us to initiate the veterans' transformation which takes time and truth.

S . . . God has set you and me apart to let the veteran and his/her family know their souls are secure.

D . . . God has designated you and me as ones who can direct the hurting one to the divine Healer.

Thank you for permission to be a bit edgy at the start of this chapter, sharing with you about the going-away party I hosted for my innards. I trust that the vignette gave you a fresh point of view on a long-standing truth: A good sense of humor and the support of trusted girlfriends are a winning combination for facing the bigger challenges we encounter in life. As you or others you know are passing through some dark place, as you learn how to manage the invisible wounds of war on the home front, we encourage you to ask God how you can be a faithful body part in the body of Christ.

Questions for Reflection

1. In your effort to cope with the stresses of combat-related PTSD in your marriage and home, have you ever found yourself pulling away from friends and social activities?

   If so, did you consciously decide to withdraw or did you unconsciously, slowly depart from your social life?

If so, why did you pull away from your friends and family?

Did this help or hurt you in your effort to endure?

2. At what point did you realize that your situation is not unique, that you are not alone in the challenges that you currently face?

How did this realization make you feel?

3. Looking back over the seasons of my life, I can see how God has been faithful to provide friends—sisters in Christ—along the way, especially in the rough stretches. A few are lifelong friends, but most have been what I call bridges, those girl-friends who came into my life for a specific season when I needed encouragement, support, and hope.

Has this been your experience too?

If so, describe a specific gift of friendship God has given to you to bridge an intense PTSD season in your life.

What qualities made her valuable to you?

4. Do you have a favorite song, Bible verse, quote, or joke about the value and power of friendships/girlfriends? What is it?

9

Permission to Engage

Spiritual Warfare on the Home Front

> Finally, be strong in the Lord and in his mighty
> power. Put on the full armor of God, so that you
> can take your stand against the devil's schemes.
>
> Ephesians 6:10–11

The room was full of chatty women on the kick-off morning of the new fall Bible study. The flurry of activity that swirled from the entrance and weaved its way around theme-decorated tables toward the podium and back again made my head swim. I stood in the back, scanning the room. I finally spotted an empty chair on the perimeter and dragged my tired body to it. The round table of women, already fully engaged in energetic conversation, obviously knew one another.

I was the new kid on the block, still rolling in the physical fatigue and emotional wake of Military Move #10. I sat there in a palpable fog, too tired to form a complete sentence. The room started to rotate slowly. I was exhausted to the bone. I was a soldier fresh from the front lines, back inside the wire for resupply. I had finally found my way back to "the rear with the gear" in hope of having my wounds cleansed and bandaged. I desperately needed to find some much needed refreshment in order to return to the front lines of life in our PTSD-affected home.

We bowed our heads to open with prayer. Behind my eyelids, an image of myself formed. I imagined what I looked like in the spirit. I was smudged and smeared with the stains of the previous weeks. A broken chin strap swung from my helmet. My canteen was empty. My shield was missing. I dragged my heavy sword behind me. My spirit staggered, coughed, and then collapsed at this table.

The prayer ended and we raised our heads again. I looked around and no longer saw a room full of chatty, cheerful women, but of weary, wounded warriors in need of triage. I looked right through their Bible study busyness and saw their bruises and their bleeding wounds caused by the enemy's assaults on them last week, last night, and this very morning. I sank into my chair, thirsty for just a sip of living water. I waited for the Word to wash over our battle wounds and for the Spirit of God to resupply our rations. We would surely be sent to the front lines again soon.

Defining Spiritual Battles on the Home Front

Post-traumatic stress disorder has also been called post-traumatic *SOUL* disorder. Because we are a trinity of body, mind, and *spirit*, our approach to psychological wounds and disorders *must* include an honest discussion about spiritual matters as they relate to PTSD. Many Christian physicians, psychologists, social workers, and ministers believe that PTSD is not only a mental wound, but equally, or even more so, a *spiritual* wound as well. Trauma of any kind can cause a fissure in the soul of a man or woman. They believe that the fissure, or opening, is a place where darkness in its many forms can either influence or infiltrate the spirit and soul of a person, depending on that person's relationship with Jesus Christ.

We readily accept that bodily wounds deserve proper examination, cleansing, repair, and rehabilitation by trained medical professionals. We don't hesitate to consult a physician for a broken bone or a deep laceration. We are not as quick to tend to a broken spirit or a hemorrhaging soul, our own or those of the ones we love, even though these unseen wounds need the same attention by informed courageous Christians. We tend to try every remedy offered in self-help books or on counselors' couches before we will consult the Physician and Healer concerning matters of the soul. Many believers, including those in leadership with medical and theological degrees, steer clear of any conversation about the relationship between mental health issues and dark spiritual activity. One reason is that our deeper convictions and stronger emotions surface when we try to come to terms with the truth about the unseen realm.

We purposely explored compassion fatigue and burnout prior to this discussion about our unseen battles in the spiritual realm because we recognize the truth of the saying, *"Fatigue makes cowards of us all."*[1] We cannot hold our ground or invade the enemy's camp if we are weak and worn out. We must take decisive steps toward basic strength training in all areas of our lives, to break the downward spiral of compassion fatigue before we can see the battlefield clearly and engage in spiritual warfare on behalf of our warriors and our families.

We believe spiritual warfare lies at the heart of the PTSD challenge. Dr. Edward Tick, author of *War and the Soul*, wrote, "We must become aware of the spiritual dimension of war, for therein lies its great power over us."[2] A Christ-centered resource would be incomplete without a basic look at spiritual activity in the lives and relationships of PTSD sufferers, more specifically spiritual activity in the lives of veterans and their family members in the aftermath of war. We will do so, looking at it through the lens of scriptural truth and teaching, in the authority and armor that God has given to each of His own.

Spiritual warfare expert, seasoned believer, and author of *The Adversary: The Christian vs. Demonic Activity* and several other books on the topic, Mark I. Bubeck, DMin, graciously provided an interview for the purposes of this chapter. He, too, believes that trauma can be the beginning of dark spiritual activity in anyone's life. He states, "I believe it is true that a personal wound through severe trauma can be an opening for the deceptive work of Satan and his kingdom. They seek to take advantage of a wounded person in myriads of ways.

"However, it's not the wound itself, but rather the lies and wrong thoughts that evil powers implant within the person about the trauma that destroy. Negative thoughts regarding God, the wounded person's self-worth, other persons in the wounded one's life, or any one of a number of responses to the trauma that do not line up with God's revelation recorded in His Word are the real dangers. Healing and restoration come as the trauma is able to be viewed in harmony with God's goodness, love, sovereign purposes, and right to shepherd our lives in any way He may choose. Our Lord never violates His attributes and divine character. He is always the 'Truth.'"

Spiritual Invasion of the Home Front

Satan is not in hell, yet. He daily roams through the earth and goes back and forth in it (see Job 1:6–7).

My son has nightmares every night. He yells, screams, and wails in his sleep. Sometimes he wakes up from them. Sometimes I have to talk to him, call to him, and try to wake him. He wakes up startled, overwhelmed with fear, soaked in sweat. He dreads the night now and finds it almost impossible to rest. He knows that his fears are waiting for him when he shuts his eyes.

I was so scared. My husband popped two sleeping pills into his mouth and washed them down with a shot of whiskey (his fourth or fifth). Then he stood at the kitchen sink, gripping the counter with both hands and started shouting commands to his men in the field. He was in the throes of battle, giving direct orders to his company and screaming at the enemy. This went on for what felt like an eternity. The worst (and best) part was that we had guests at the time. Nothing we said or did could bring him back to the present. It took two men to pry my husband's hands from the kitchen sink and to escort him to the bed. He collapsed and slept until morning. When he woke up, he remembered nothing about the episode.

In an instant, his mood changes. One time something triggered him and he raised his fist over my head. I covered myself as best I could. Then he smashed a glass serving dish onto the granite counter and another onto the kitchen floor.

We were in his car driving home from dinner when he started yelling and cursing at me at the top of his lungs. His driving was dangerous and out of control. He slammed his fist into the steering wheel over and over, screaming at me to go to hell and taking God's name in vain repeatedly. I told him to stop the car and to let me get out. He didn't. I was trapped in the moving vehicle with him as he threatened me verbally and physically for more than forty-five minutes.

He threatened to kill me. He said he had killed before and he would do it again.

151

Have you ever considered that you might be dealing with the devil? Have you ever wondered whether you and your family are experiencing what the apostle Paul described as "spiritual forces of evil in the heavenly realms"[3] on your home front? Behind those confusing, divisive, and painful interactions within your most cherished relationships a grueling wrestling match may be taking place with something or someone unseen.

We who love and live with a combat veteran can attest to the fact that war has literally come home. But that is a polite way of saying that after the honeymoon phase of the veterans' homecomings, the collateral damage of war blew up our marriages, families, and dreams.

The truth is that war is a living, breathing beast with legs that arrogantly stride through our living rooms, with muddy feet that stomp down our hallways, and with clenched fists that beat, break, and bruise. War is a being with a boisterous, violent voice and a voracious appetite for human souls on the home front. War is never satiated by signed treaties or surrenders. The silence of the guns and battlefields is deceiving. The fight isn't over; it simply changed addresses.

Reliable resources help us attribute many of the signs and symptoms of PTSD to the proven physiological explanations for our loved one's behaviors and choices. However, because science cannot soothe the soul, some of the variables in the home front equation don't add up. The spiritual component is an enigma that begs to differ with science, with what can be seen, touched, measured, and repeated in laboratories. Professionals scratch their heads, shrug their shoulders, and chalk up the unexplained and unseen as another mental health mystery.

Family members of combat veterans readily admit they believe much is going on behind what the eye can detect.

I can clearly see that it is a spiritual war going on when it comes to the PTSD.

I am aware that Satan would like nothing better than to destroy my warrior, my family, and me.

After we began a stronger effort to battle the PTSD and join with a couple to mentor us spiritually, I became more aware of the spiritual attacks on our family.

I tend to be the prayer cover for him and our children. Through his experiences, he has constructed some inner mixed and misconstrued thoughts about Christianity, religions, and belief systems in general.

Yes, absolutely. I know we are dealing with spiritual warfare!

This was a new discovery and understanding for me.

I firmly believe that we are always at war with the satanic realm. If you are a believer and if you seek to serve the Lord, you will be targeted by satanic forces.

Allowing for a spiritual dimension influences the way we approach the challenges of invisible wounds on the home front. First, it influences how we identify and deal with our loved one's symptoms. It can change our approach to conflict resolution in our closest relationships. It has great bearing on how we learn to manage our thought patterns. And, finally, it can determine how we will respond to the chronic stress.

Pray for Discernment

The symptoms of PTSD and TBI, such as flashbacks, triggers, violence, rage, depression, and suicidal ideation or attempts are recognized as psychological and mental responses to abnormal, prolonged stress and the traumatic experience. Distinguishing between what is physical, psychological, and spiritual in nature has historically been a huge challenge. Discerning between what is a psychological/physiological symptom and what is simply the warrior's choice of response or behavior and what is a spiritual attack is an ability only God can provide fully. The signs and symptoms of PTSD and other disorders are a part of mental health problems and don't always have a spiritual source. Also, a believer can choose to use satanic weapons, such as lying, stealing, anger, and profanity[4] against another believer or against himself. This is a gray area; therefore it is important to understand that spiritual warfare can also be involved.

According to Warren Wiersbe, "We sometimes suffer simply because we are human. . . . Not all suffering is Satanic in origin . . . But there is a kind of suffering that is Satan's weapon and that is what Job experienced."[5] The devil exploits our minds whether we are healthy or injured, and he specializes in targeting our vulnerabilities. These wounded places of the soul can become beachheads, places from which the invading spiritual army can operate and can move deeper into the territory in order to take higher ground. Every situation presents a unique set of physical, emotional, and spiritual elements.

Spiritual warfare is not something to undertake alone, ever. And it requires preparation. Only a fool rides out into battle without preparation, training, or knowledge of the battlefield.

The first and most important step in gaining discernment is to be steeped in the Word of God, which has the power to divide matters of soul and spirit. "For the word of God is alive and active. Sharper than any double-edged sword, it penetrates even to dividing soul and spirit, joints and marrow; it judges the thoughts and attitudes of the heart."[6] Only then can we begin to recognize enemy activity for what it is.

Chris and Rahnella Adsit, coauthors of *When War Comes Home: Christ-Centered Healing for Wives of Combat Veterans*, state:

The war in your home is being fought on three fronts: physical, mental and spiritual. It's absolutely vital to use tactics that meet each threat strategically. Physical difficulties that you or your husband are experiencing need physical solutions; mental/emotional difficulties require psychological approaches; spiritual attacks necessitate spiritual defenses and counter-attacks. Our enemy will often utilize a combination of all three fronts in his efforts to bring us down, but we must be discerning enough to differentiate between them. . . . Your adversary is the devil—not your husband! Anyone who lives with a reactive, angry, irritable, belligerent and emotionally draining person might feel a natural tendency to become somewhat adversarial. . . . Feelings of disappointment and betrayal flow easily into the vacuum. . . . Before you know it, you've got your cross hairs on your husband's back, and your trigger-finger is getting itchy. It's at such moments that you need to realize that he is not your enemy! In every sense of the word, he is a victim of the enemy's attacks—just as you are. Better that you should stand shoulder-to-shoulder fighting your enemy together.[7]

PTSD or a Prowling Lion

Be self-controlled and alert. Your enemy the devil prowls around like a roaring lion looking for someone to devour. Resist him, standing firm in the faith (1 Peter 5:8–9 NIV 1984).

Many of the manifestations of PTSD can mimic sin, or "acts of the flesh." Paul's list in Galatians 5:19–22 sounds much like PTSD on the home front: "sexual immorality, impurity and debauchery; idolatry and witchcraft; hatred, discord, jealousy, fits of rage, selfish ambition, dissensions, factions and envy; drunkenness, orgies, and the like." How can you discern between signs of the disorder and spiritual rebellion? A closer look at some of these acts of the flesh that are particular to PTSD is important.

The War Chest

Articles of war that are looked at as souvenirs can become idols or destructive in the home. We don't want to sound crazy about this, but we want to emphasize that we should exercise caution. Examples of war chest items are expended ordinance or shell casings, rifles, pistols and knives that were used in battle, captured flags, enemy uniforms or personal effects, or any other spoils of war. They can have the potential of becoming idols if they become a source of sinful pride or a boost to one's ego. God told the Israelites time and again not to take any plunder from their conquests for themselves. Many times in Scripture, God commanded that these spoils be dedicated to the building up of His house. If His people disobeyed, the consequences weren't pretty. Anything that we put before God or anything that takes away from our worship of God is an idol. Ask: Am I worshiping violence when I look at that object? Am I glorifying or exalting myself by displaying or treasuring this item? Can I truly look at the item as what it is, that it simply represents something from that country and nothing more?

Substance Abuse

Prescription and illegal drug abuse as well as alcohol abuse are rampant among veterans who suffer with PTSD. The Greek word for witchcraft is *pharmakeia*, which is defined as "the use of the administering of drugs, poisoning, sorcery, magical arts, often found in connection with idolatry and fostered by it."[8] The word is found five times in the New Testament, once in Galatians and four times in Revelation.[9] *Pharmakeia* gives Satan and wicked spirits a beachhead, a foothold. The enemy can take advantage of the misuse of alcohol and drugs to infiltrate a person's mind, heart, will, and personality and it can extend to the veteran's family and work relationships.

Satan is a thief.[10] The abuse or misuse of medications for chronic pain and sleep aids as well as the abuse of alcohol and illegal drugs can steal one's ability to be rational and can change the way one's mind operates. These substances are addictive and can take away one's power of choice and self-control. Prescribed medications, alcohol, and illegal drugs can become beachheads for the powers of darkness to gain a foothold. When the original pain transitions into something more chronic, the veteran is now suffering. When the prescription or substance becomes the means of managing the suffering, it can transition into an addiction. That's when the substance becomes a thief and robs the veteran of the ability to manage the problem on his/her own. When a veteran or family member becomes dependent on the substance to usher in relief, Satan has achieved his goal.

"Drugs or alcohol are related to *pharmakeia* or sorcery and witchcraft. Anything that dulls one's ability to be in control of his body, thoughts, and emotions makes that person more subject to the devil's deceptions and schemes to get one to do more to allow demonic control. That gives ground to demonic control that needs one to reclaim the ground by going through a careful process like The Steps To Freedom outlined in *The Bondage Breaker,* by Neil T. Anderson. Giving in to addictions opens one's life to serious problems that may need the help of programs like Alcoholics Anonymous for support for a season."[11]

Rulers, Authorities, and Powers

> For our struggle is not against flesh and blood, but against the rulers, against the authorities, against the powers of this dark world and against the spiritual forces of evil in the heavenly realms (Ephesians 6:12).

Many believers assert that the geographic location and spiritual history of battlefields can affect the spiritual health and faith of our warriors while they are in-country. They refer to the prophet Daniel's encounter with heaven's angelic envoy and the angel's description of his being delayed three weeks by a battle with the spiritual "prince of the Persian kingdom."[12] Some assert that the darkness of a geographic location can spiritually attach itself to the warriors, to their person and to their belongings with which they return home. This subject is much too large for us to cover appropriately here. However, this is an issue of concern that the Christian community should squarely face and prayerfully address.

Nightmares and Night Terrors

You will not fear the terror of night (Psalm 91:5).

Dreams happen. They are an important part of our sleep cycle when we have rapid eye movement. It is during the REM cycle that we experience the replenishing nourishment to our physical bodies. Dreams are simply raw emotion with no parameters for reality.

An unpleasant dream comes with strong negative emotions of fear, horror, danger, terror, and discomfort. We awaken distressed and can't return to sleep for a while.[13] Warriors dream about battle scenes, a dead friend, the faces of dead bodies, putting a dead friend into a body bag, or a collage of unrelated disturbing experiences. These unpleasant dreams, or nightmares, are horrifying, suspenseful, and have a great deal of despair and anxiety involved. The warrior senses a loss of control or great danger.

In his interview for this book, Dr. Mark Bubeck told us,

Nightmares are also a vital subject to handle with prayerful and careful spiritual care. The major issue remains one's personal, saving relationship to our Lord Jesus Christ. Prayer practices are always helpful and important but unless "new birth" is a reality in a person's life, protective prayer practices will not be as long-lasting and effective.

I have found that prayers before one goes to sleep are so important. The Round-Up Prayer[14] is a helpful prayer tool to present one's whole person to the Lord Jesus Christ and to resist attempts of powers to tamper with any aspect of our person. God has used that daily practice to help many in dealing with dream issues.

In addition, a prayer of this type can be a wonderful assist just before one goes to sleep: "In the name of my Lord Jesus Christ and by the power of His blood, I place all of my dream capacities under the shepherding care of my Lord Jesus Christ while I sleep. I ask my Savior to protect me from all evil powers' attempts to torment me in my dreams with terror and other evil designs that may come from past experiences or traumas. In Jesus' name, I forbid evil powers to afflict and control my dreams in any way. I look to my Lord Jesus Christ to enable me to rest in Him and His finished work. Amen."

I have seen prayers like this completely stop tormenting nightmares. It is important not to forget. Pray it each night before going to sleep. Evil powers are always on the alert to take advantage of our failure to keep such important things under our Lord's protective care. After having done this faithfully, and one has a disturbing dream, the moment one awakens, it is good to pray: "Lord Jesus Christ, You know I had this disturbing dream and I ask You now to bring to my mind Your purpose in my having this dream. If there is something I need to deal with related to this dream, please bring it to my mind." That's an important part of allowing the Lord to shepherd your life. I have seen important insights granted that may have to do with the need to ask the Lord to reclaim ground given in past sinful practices. A faithful wife can help her husband pray in such a pattern or if necessary, to do it for him.

Prayer is prayer. It's not a matter of "he can't" pray, but that the warrior is inhibited. So we pray for the warrior to be released. This is part of the reclaiming of territory that was given over, consciously or not, to the enemy previously.

Abdication of Spiritual Leadership

> But I want you to realize that the head of every man is Christ, and the head of the woman is man, and the head of Christ is God (1 Corinthians 11:3).

Sometimes in PTSD-affected marriages, the warrior abdicates his role as spiritual head of the home, stops taking the lead in spiritual matters, vows never to set foot in church again, and questions faith, doctrine, and the Bible. The result is that wives and children of many PTSD sufferers are spiritually naked, literally "uncovered" in the spiritual realm, because the wife has lost her spiritual covering or "head." First and most importantly, the woman needs to know that when her man has moved away from his God-given responsibility, Christ becomes her Head and she assumes the role of priestess in her home. Second, seasoned believers need to step into the gap to provide prayer, protection, and guidance.

Permission to Engage

> For though we live in the world, we do not wage war as the world does. The weapons we fight with are not the weapons of the world. On the contrary, they have divine power to demolish strongholds. We demolish arguments and every pretension that sets itself up against the knowledge of God, and we take captive every thought to make it obedient to Christ. . . . You are looking only on the surface of things (2 Corinthians 10:3–5, 7 NIV 1984).

A news headline caught my attention recently. A young woman at home alone with her baby heard an intruder trying to break through her front door. She grabbed her loaded gun with one hand and called 9-1-1 to alert the authorities of her situation with her other hand. She repeatedly asked the dispatcher a critical question:
"If he comes through the door, can I shoot him?"

When the enemy invades, God has already given us permission to do something about it. Spiritual warfare is not a spectator sport. It is a full-contact activity. We have been given authority to *do* something when the enemy invades our turf. Jesus Christ has already said, "I have given you authority to trample on snakes and scorpions and to overcome all the power of the enemy; nothing will harm you."[15] Jesus has given us authority over every evil spiritual activity that takes place in our lives, and in the lives of our loved ones and our fellow believers. There are proactive steps and defensive measures we can take daily on behalf of our loved ones even after they have given ground over to the other side.

This chapter cannot possibly contain or even mention all the powerful, well-researched resources available to you on this subject. We can only give you the basics, a spiritual boot camp. As a starting point for you in this area of following Christ, we offer the ABCs of spiritual warfare on the home front.

A. Acknowledge the spiritual element in home front conflicts.

B. Believe God and what He has said about who you are and about the weapons, tactics, and targets used by your spiritual enemies.

C. Clothe yourself in Christ and in the full armor of God and communicate with your Commander-in-Chief continuously.

A. Acknowledge the spiritual element in your home front conflicts. The turning point for me was working through *The Steps to Freedom in Christ*, a booklet by Neil T. Anderson. This step-by-step process helped me learn to engage in the spiritual war on my own home front. It has been used by hundreds of thousands to discover their victory as children of God. "Being open to every step of this process and becoming aware of any ground we've given to the enemy is the first step," Bubeck says.

B. Believe God and what He has said about who you are and about the weapons, tactics, and targets used by your spiritual enemies. Identifying and believing the truths of Scripture, focusing the Word of God on your loved ones, protecting them, and warring for them in the Spirit is the next step toward victory on the home front. Dr. Bubeck and others emphasize the importance of memorizing God's promises and even longer portions of the Word and whole psalms. "Ask God for the ability to memorize so that you will be armed and ready at any given moment. I suggest Romans 8; Hebrews 12; Psalms 27, 46, 86, 91, and 139 as basics toward spiritual health, freedom and joy."

C. Clothe yourself in Christ and in the full armor of God. The truth is most people leave home spiritually naked every day. If we had spiritual eyes to see that, I believe we would insist on taking measures to get properly dressed in the Spirit before our feet hit the floor. An excerpt from *Hope for the Home Front: Winning the Emotional and Spiritual Battles of a Military Wife* explains how to get dressed:

My husband is not the only soldier in this family. I, too, am enlisted in the ranks. My battles, however, belong not to this nation, but to the Lord, "For the battle is not yours, but God's" (2 Chronicles 20:15). While my warrior invades tangible enemy turf by sea, air, and land, I engage the invisible opposition on my knees. Because my Commander knows how brutal the battlefield of temptation can be, He has issued combat gear, divinely designed for my spiritual, physical, and emotional protection.

Before my feet hit the floor, I am wise to dress daily for war. Ephesians 6:13–17 inventories the protective gear at my disposal, "Therefore put on the full armor of God, so that when the day of evil comes, you may be able to stand your ground, and after you have done everything, to stand. Stand firm then, with the belt of truth buckled around your waist, with the breastplate of righteousness in place, and with your feet fitted with the readiness that comes from the gospel of peace. In addition to all this, take up the shield of faith, with which you can extinguish all the flaming arrows of the evil one. Take the helmet of salvation and the sword of the Spirit, which is the word of God."

If I hastily start my day, entering the war zone with just one piece of armor loosely fitted, unkempt, or missing, my foe will undoubtedly target the vulnerable vital part. His prowess guarantees a bull's-eye. The arrow pierces and I, a wounded warrior, am crippled, unable to stand "against the devil's schemes" (Ephesians 6:11). Then, throughout my day, I fight ineffectively, suffer multiple injuries, and frantically limp in retreat from his onslaught. At the same time, my family and friends experience heavy casualties because I am rendered incompetent to hold the line and fight alongside them.

Defeat is avoidable when I wisely clothe myself in the armor God offers. Once I have slipped on my helmet and boots, tightened my belt and breastplate, and raised my shield, I am protected from any toxic spears Satan may hurl at me. A trained soldier doesn't just stand unarmed in the crossfire. A true warrior grasps a deadly weapon and sounds the charge. God arms us for this advance by giving us the sword of the Spirit, His powerful Word, the only offensive weapon listed in His inventory.

The sword—"the word of God is living and active. Sharper than any double-edged sword, it penetrates even to dividing soul and spirit, joints and marrow; it judges the thoughts and attitudes of the heart" (Hebrews 4:12). Jesus even demonstrated proper handling of this weapon for us when He was confronted by the tempter at the beginning of His earthly ministry. Jesus met all three temptations with Scripture, the truth all believers have at their disposal. Our arsenals are full of heavenly hand grenades, godly guns, master missiles, and all kinds of almighty artillery with which we can disarm, disintegrate, and defeat all the hostile armies that flank us.

Communicate with Your Commander-in-Chief Continuously

One of Satan's biggest fears is to see the smallest believer on her knees. Commit to a daily time of prayer, intercession, and worship, just you and God. Pray alone. Pray also with partners on a regular basis. Learn from others who are seasoned prayer warriors. Dr. Bubeck suggests supporting the traumatized person by doctrinal praying in their behalf and enlisting the person's participation, if he or she is willing. Teach your warrior how to pray doctrinal prayers by giving him or her copies and a challenge to memorize prayers in the Word, like 1 Peter 1:3–9 and Hebrews 12:1–15. He says, "Pray silently in the long periods of poor communication and feeling stuck. Pray in the midst of a crisis on the home front, big or small. My first suggestion is a doctrinal prayer tool approach to war against the evidences manifested that suggest possible demonic activity such as anger, rage, fear, hate, etc. Use this prayer several times each day to battle in behalf of your veteran against the spirits troubling him/her by naming them and taking authority over them. This can be done in silent prayer or when the situation permits, by audible verbalized prayer."

Learn to pray the Scriptures for yourself, your veteran, your children, your trials. We recommend using doctrinal prayers found in resources such as *Prayers that Avail Much* (Harrison House, 1980), THE POWER OF A PRAYING (wife, husband, parent, etc.) series by Stormie Omartian (Harvest House Publishers, 2007), and "A Daily Prayer for Freedom" in *Waking the Dead* by John Eldredge (Thomas Nelson, 2006).

The next step is prayer to break barriers, walls, and relationships that the kingdom of darkness is building between the warrior and the loved ones. Believers have the authority to pull those down. Dr. Bubeck suggests using this powerful prayer silently in the midst of any situation on the home front. Use it often and you will see great benefit. When you don't know what to say, use the suggested prayers in the following section.

A Crisis Prayer Suggestion

In crisis situations where you suspect degrees of demonic bondage in your own life or the life of one close to you, the following procedures have brought release and freedom:

Set aside one day a week for fasting and prayer. Enlist others who may share your spiritual burden and concern. Pray a brief doctrinal prayer of this kind each hour on the hour:

"In the name of my Lord Jesus Christ and by the power of His blood, I pull down all deceptive powers of darkness seeking to deceive and control (name the person) by (name the symptoms). I command these powers of darkness to cease their wicked work and they must leave (name the person) and go where my Lord Jesus Christ sends them."

Continue to use this practice until relief is evident or until more direct and personal help is possible. Whenever you sense barriers or stressed relationships with your warrior or your loved ones, pray:

"In the name of my Lord Jesus Christ and by the power of His blood, I pull down all barriers and relationships between (name the person) and me that are being authored by Satan and the powers of darkness. I ask my Lord Jesus Christ to build relationships between (name the person) and me that are authored by the Holy Spirit in the will of God."

God has given us, His children, the privilege of prayer and has provided us with the protective spiritual armor to keep us standing effectively on the home front. This knowledge and discernment must then be applied to our unique set of challenges. We need to recognize the role that medications and modern treatment options and therapies have in the recovery of our loved one's physical and psychological health. The meds and the therapies have value.

As we learn to apply the truths of God's Word to our circumstances, He will give us the discernment to find and maintain balance between respecting the guidance of physicians and psychologists in matters of physical and mental health. God will also help us discern the difference between mental, physical, and spiritual issues. It is important to follow our physicians' and therapists' advice, take prescribed medications for chronic pain and chemical imbalances properly, and at the same time respond to the work of the adversary in our life and in the lives of our loved ones. However, the use of balanced spiritual warfare is always in order. And, in those teachable, tender moments, when the door to our warrior's heart and mind is open and listening, we can encourage his or her intimacy with the Lord, but not to the exclusion of prescribed medical treatment.

I pray. I ask for help, strength, and wisdom. I also pray over my husband, for his physical, mental, and spiritual well-being.

I try to do the best I can, but usually after conflicts I end up turning to prayer and asking God for help and guidance for whatever the particular situation is.

I ask for wisdom to know how to approach my husband and deal with situations, how to discern between things he says and does and what the meaning might be behind them.

Spiritual Victory on the Home Front

Warren Wiersbe reminds us, "You are not fighting for victory but from victory, for Jesus Christ has already defeated Satan."[16] Scripture tells us that the enemy always comes to steal, kill and destroy. But the other part of that verse is the victory: Jesus has "come that [you] may have life, and have it to the full."[17] He came to earth to destroy the works of the devil and did so at the cross.

I am married to a wounded warrior who has TBI, PTSD, alcoholism, and severe health issues. I've had to deal with this entire combination on several occasions. The fire department, paramedics, and police frequent our home in time of need. I am a five-foot-three woman. My wounded warrior is five eleven. Most of the emergency responders are men that are at least six feet tall. Most of these responders seem like giants to me.

One specific day, my wounded warrior was uncontrollable. Seven emergency responders could not manage my wounded warrior. I was in battle. I was dressed with my armor of God. My helmet of salvation was protecting my head, my body was covered in my armored suit, my protective shield was in one hand, and my sword was in my other hand. I knew that I was not alone. With God's help I would be victorious. I stood strong, resisted the enemy, and shouted out the stand-down order to my wounded warrior. The battle was over. The war had been won. My wounded warrior was back to reality. Praise the Lord! The emergency responders were able to do their job and transport my wounded warrior to the hospital for medical assistance. As I was reminded of David's battle with Goliath, God was indeed with me.

I work hard at taking my thoughts captive and giving them to God. During the times when I especially feel like it is a spiritual attack, I sometimes have to do this even on an hourly basis. I try not to let my thoughts defeat me.

Our mentor couple came to pray over our home with us. They anointed every doorway with oil and prayed over each and every room in our home with us. After that I felt a special anointing over our home and family. I get a sense of the strongest angels battling the dark, difficult battles on our behalf. Sometimes I just get a sense to pray, often I don't really even know for what specifically, but I do. Our home getting blessed is just one of the stances we have taken against spiritual darkness in our lives.

Questions for Reflection

1. Have you, as a family member of a veteran with PTSD, ever considered that you are dealing with "spiritual forces of evil

in the heavenly realms" on your home front (see Ephesians 6:12)?

2. If so, how has this perspective influenced the way you approach the PTSD challenges on your home front, such as

- Identifying and dealing with your loved one's symptoms

- Dealing with conflict in your closest relationships

- Managing your thought life

- Choosing how you will respond to the chronic stress?

3. Have you experienced a specific spiritual victory (small or big) that you would be willing to describe and share?

If so, why was it a victory?

10

The Savior's War Wounds: Our Hope

> Even now my witness is in heaven; my advocate
> is on high. My intercessor is my friend as my
> eyes pour out tears to God; on behalf of a man
> he pleads with God as one pleads for a friend.
>
> Job 16:19–21

Jenna couldn't seem to sit still. Her older brother and sister were nestled into the pew in their Sunday garb, content to color quietly while the preacher's voice rose and fell. Not three-year-old Jenna. Somewhere between points one and two of the preacher's three-point sermon, Jenna let us all know that she was thoroughly bored with the formalities and that the contents of her "big church bag," a collection of crayons, coloring books, and candy, weren't cutting it that particular Sunday morning.

She fidgeted and fussed. Mark gently pried her chubby fingers from the hymnal, Bible, and offering envelopes, which she had removed for the third time, and returned the books and papers to their proper slots. She studied his stern expression. Although she read him loud and clear, she proceeded to slide off the pew to the floor and to climb back up a dozen times. Each time on her way down, the heels of her black patent leather shoes clicked on the floor. She liked that. On her way up, she strained, gasped, grunted, coughed, and sighed for attention.

Mark lifted her to his lap. Her saucer-sized blue eyes studied his face again for a fraction of a minute. Then she suddenly threw her arms straight over her head and arched her back to launch herself from his lap. In one fluid movement, he intercepted her tiny tantrum midair, scooped her diapered bottom into his arms, stood up, and made his way toward the aisle and the woodshed. Her blond curls swung right and left as she shot panicked looks at her brother, her sister, and then me. Realizing the physical fight was futile, the verbal bargaining began.

"I be good, I be good, I be good, Daddy," she pleaded softly to her father, cupping his chin with both of her little hands and batting her eyelashes. He made it to the aisle and turned toward the double doors that led to the foyer.

"I be good, I be good, I be good, Daddy," her appeal got louder and more distressed. Her father kept stride. Heads turned as people's attention moved from the pulpit to the preschooler headed for punishment. The preacher paused. The congregation snickered.

"I be good, Daddy, I be good, I be good!" She hollered her final petitions just as Mark pushed the swinging doors open and stepped into the foyer. When she realized something very unpleasant and painful was imminent, she appealed to a higher court.

"HEP ME, JEEEEESUUUUUUSSSSSS!" she flung her final desperate words toward the altar before the doors swung shut. Her plea reverberated through the church.

Laughter erupted from the congregation, which had completely lost its composure. The pastor wisely recognized the teachable moment at hand. Instead of returning to his sermon, he allowed Jenna's plea for mercy and pardon to preach for itself.

Tests, Trials, Temptations, and Fiery Ordeals

When the writers of Scripture spoke about the difficulties of life, they carefully selected several different Hebrew and Greek words, depending on the point they aimed to make. James confirms this careful wordsmithing in his letter to the first-century Christians.

> Consider it pure joy, my brothers and sisters, whenever you face **trials of many kinds,** because you know that the testing of your faith produces perseverance. Let perseverance finish its work so that you may be mature and complete, not lacking anything (James 1:2–4, emphasis added).

These "trials of many kinds" are expressed by different original Hebrew and Greek words. The writers recognized that trials come in varying degrees of difficulty and duration and chose their words prayerfully for good reason. Most difficult times, such as tests, trials, and temptations, come and go like the ebb and flow of the ocean's tide. They gradually arrive, reach their peak, then retreat and fade until another time. Others, like the "fiery ordeals" less frequently mentioned in the Bible, arrive uninvited and stay a long, agonizing while. Instead of gradually ebbing and flowing, they smash again and again into the shoreline of our lives. They collide relentlessly against the relationships we cherish, and over time they threaten to erode the very foundations of family and faith. This kind of suffering, like the lingering effects of war, seems to have no end in sight and is full of *"Hep me, Jesus"* moments for both the warrior and his or her loved ones.

James tells us to "count it pure joy whenever you face trials of many kinds," including the fiery ordeals veterans and the veterans' families inevitably encounter following the combat experience.

We can count it all joy only because we know that the pain is not pointless, but is infused with God's purpose to complete and perfect us. Trials are one of the tools He chooses to do so.

Trials don't produce faith; trials *prove* our faith to be genuine. Scripture tells us that Jesus authors faith in us and that hearing the Word of God makes our faith productive. Trials produce patience. This kind of patience is not like the patience necessary to tolerate traffic or to be polite in a bank line or to wait for a wedding proposal. The kind of patience that our hardships, temptations, and persecutions produce goes much deeper. James is referring to the physical perseverance and spiritual staying power required to complete a grueling marathon. Trials have the potential to produce this kind of tenacity in us, if we receive them with faith, rely on God's character and promises for the journey, and refuse to become bitter and discouraged no matter how long the storm hovers and rages.

Jesus faced every kind of trial that we face.[1] His temptations, hardships, and fiery ordeals resulted in visible and invisible wounds. He experienced the physical pain of bodily injuries as well as the emotional and spiritual wounds of deep sorrow and grief.[2] Scripture makes it clear that God is committed to making us like Jesus, His Son, "And we know that in all things God works for the good of those who love him, who have been called according to his purpose. For those God foreknew he also predestined to be conformed to the image of his Son, that he might be the firstborn among many brothers and sisters."[3]

Most Christians courageously quote and claim only the first half of this scriptural truth. We are very familiar with Romans 8:28: "And we know that in all things God works for the good of those who love him, who have been called according to his purpose." However, we miss the point if we stop there, in the middle of the Author's train of thought. The next verse tells us that God's purpose to which we are called is to be "conformed to the image of his Son."

God foreknew that we would one day be followers of His Son when as yet we only existed in His creative mind. Before the dawn of measured time, He declared it our destiny to be formed to the likeness of Jesus, the only one with whom God is well pleased.[4] He uses trials and tests to shape our will and our walk until they mirror those of His Son.

We prefer triumph and comfort over trials and discomfort. But in God's economy, we can't have one without the other. When James and John asked if they could sit to the right and left of Jesus' throne in heaven, he answered them with a question: "Can you drink the cup I drink?"[5] The apostle Paul expressed the same idea, "I want to know Christ—yes, to know the power of his resurrection and participation in his sufferings, becoming like him in his death, and so, somehow, attaining to the resurrection from the dead."[6]

We can "count it pure joy when we face trials of many kinds," such as the confusing words and hurtful choices of our veterans, the deep current of anger with which we wrestle, the living grief of shattered dreams, and the daily, draining spiritual battles on the home front. We know that God is working in and through, in front of and behind, over and under all our difficulties and ordeals to make us as pleasing to himself as Jesus. That's "the good" for which God is working!

Grandmother and Gethsemane

As a follower of Jesus Christ, I am learning to view life's most difficult days from the same vantage point that Jesus did on the night before the worst and last day of His earthly life. I am learning to look at the hardest days on the home front by looking at Jesus' actions in Gethsemane, the place He chose when He was in the most danger of losing hope.

"I'll meet you at the Golden Gate."

My grandmother spoke these reassuring words to me through the years when our times of belly laughter, heart connection, and tender love brushed the hem of the inevitable truth—that more than likely she, my soul mate, would reach heaven's shores before I would. In those sweet intersections of the here and now with the there and then, whenever I expressed how much I needed her in my life and never wanted to have to say goodbye, she'd reply, *"I'll meet you at the Golden Gate,"* her Irish blue eyes filled with love and faith. The last time I saw my grandmother, she lay "on the flat of her back," as she would say of others before it became her lot too. As I said my dreaded goodbyes, she exhaled in a labored whisper one last treasure for my heart to hold.

"I'll meet you at the Golden Gate."

In the year following her departure, the storms at home threatened to tear me apart. In a very dark time, feeling alone in my shattered dreams and believing there was no hope left for my marriage, I fled to her vacant home for emotional refuge in the foothills of Appalachia. I walked from room to silent room, remembering summer visits and family holiday gatherings. Finally I crumpled into the sagging couch and began to weep, praying from the hollowness of her home and from the stark emptiness of my soul to God, believing that He saw me, heard me, and could handle my loud, hard questions. Defying the devastation that was running loose on my home front, I hurled my uninhibited prayers toward heaven.

When my tirade diminished to a whimper, I quieted outwardly but not inwardly. The silence screamed back at me. I ached to hear my grandmother's voice calling from the kitchen that supper would soon be ready or to hear her slippered feet padding from room to room. I longed for her gentle touch on my shoulder and her soft-spoken, courageous intercession for me. I asked God, if it were possible, to let my grandmother know that I was there in her house, the reasons that I had sought refuge there, and that I loved and missed her so very much. Then I drifted off to sleep.

I awakened about an hour later. The setting Carolina sun streamed through the slits of the miniblinds. The light flickered around my swollen eyes until I fully opened them. I straightened up, tried to shake off the disorientation, and decided to see what, if anything, remained in her closets and cupboards. I did not set out to find dust-collecting trinkets or overlooked valuables. I simply ached to come across even a scrap of paper with her handwriting on it. I opened her bedroom closet. The shelves were bare except for a small stack of papers and spiral notebooks. I flipped through the notebooks hoping to find one of her countless journals. Empty. I transferred the papers to the bed where I could spread them out in the light and sort through them. I found a few articles torn from magazines, a picture of Jesus cut from a greeting card, and a five-by-seven photo. I turned the photo over and was stunned by what I saw. It was a faded photograph of Old Jerusalem's Golden Gate on the eastern side of the Temple Mount. It had been taken by my grandmother from the adjacent hill, the Mount of Olives, from the Garden of Gethsemane.

I couldn't breathe. Tears welled up in my eyes. One thing was certain and this one thing was all that mattered: I was uncertain where God was in all the hell our home front had become; but God knew exactly where *I* was, physically, mentally, and spiritually, before I had begun to pray. He had patiently listened to every word of my disjointed, desperate cries that had bordered on disrespect and unbelief. He saw me. He heard me in my life's most unattractive, hysterical "Hep me, Jesus" moment ever. I held the photo of the Golden Gate in my trembling hands, the faded image blurring and distorting through my tears. I wept tears of relief born of the simple, yet profound realization that God had met me right where I was.

The Gift of Gethsemane

The Garden of Gethsemane was to Jesus what Grandmother's house was to me, a place of refuge that offered a glimpse of eternity.

That spot on the side of a humble hill held great significance in the life of our Savior. He went there often with His disciples to rest. He went to the Mount of Olives, where Gethsemane is located, every night of His final week on earth.[7] Jesus was in emotional agony at Gethsemane on the night of His arrest. He stared down His worst nightmare in that garden. After His resurrection and the forty days with His disciples, He ascended from the highest point of that garden, from the top of the Mount of Olives, and sat down at the right hand of God.[8] Zechariah prophesied that when Jesus returns for us, His feet will stand right where they left our planet, atop the Mount of Olives at the edge of Gethsemane, and the mountain will split in half.[9] And it is from this very place that Jesus' coronation celebration and eternal reign will begin, as He walks the path down the Mount of Olives, through the Garden of Gethsemane, and up toward the Golden Gate, also known as the Eastern Gate, of Jerusalem, into the holy Temple as King of Kings and Lord of Lords!

It was in Gethsemane that He firmly cautioned His disciples to "pray so that you will not fall into temptation."[10] He knew there would come a day in their lives, too, just as in ours, when they would face their greatest nightmare and be tempted to lose hope. And it was from the highest rock at the edge of Gethsemane that He reassured them that great joy would follow their season of mourning: "Go into all the world and preach the gospel to all creation. Whoever believes and is baptized will be saved, but whoever does not believe will be condemned. And these signs will accompany those who believe: In my name they will drive out demons; they will speak in new tongues; they will pick up snakes with their hands; and when they drink deadly poison, it will not hurt them at all; they will place their hands on sick people, and they will get well."[11]

It's no coincidence that the times Jesus spent in this garden bookended His greatest battle. On the darkest night of His soul, His hot tears fell on the stones as He begged His Father on bended knee for a different plan. On the brightest morning of His life, nearly six weeks later, His feet left the rocky Mount of Olives when He was taken up into heaven in full view of His disciples.

Every veteran and every veteran's family member need a personal Gethsemane, a place of refuge that offers a glimpse of eternity. Our personal Gethsemane is that place where we choose to seek God, to offer up our most excruciating questions in faith, believing that nothing is too difficult for God. Our Gethsemane is that place where we make the decision to trust the Healer, the One who promises to work all things together for good.

Between the bookends of the agony and the glory of His times in Gethsemane, Jesus suffered visible and invisible wounds on our behalf. The prophet Isaiah wrote, "But he was pierced for our transgressions, he was crushed for our iniquities; the punishment that brought us peace was on him, and by his wounds we are healed."[12] Jesus' disciple Peter wrote, "'He himself bore our sins' in his body on the cross, so that we might die to sins and live for righteousness; 'by his wounds you have been healed.'"[13]

Remember, God is committed to conforming us to the image of His Son. Suffering is a step in the process of being conformed to Christ. Jesus suffered; therefore we, His followers, can expect to experience situations that rock us to the very core of our being. We can count it all joy, not only that we are becoming more like His perfect Son, not only that God will be faithful to comfort us and supply our need, but that He will use us as His "wounded healers" in the realm and reach of our individual influence. Only those who have hurt deeply and experienced personally the compassion and comfort of the Creator can compassionately comfort others who hurt.

Praise be to the God and Father of our Lord Jesus Christ, the Father of compassion and the God of all comfort, who comforts us in all our troubles, so that we can comfort those in any trouble with the comfort we ourselves receive from God (2 Corinthians 1:3–4).

His desire is that we trust Him and take Him at His word, even when we are staring our worst and longest nightmare in the face. He is in the process of making us a powerful conduit and example of His Son. God will be faithful to redeem the very place where our hottest tears have fallen as long as they fall in faith that He is up to something good. The wounded can be of special service to God, for they have compassion for those He is calling to himself. God will anoint His injured own and call us to bring "relief and deliverance" for "such a time as this" in the lives of others.[14]

As we trust His wisdom, acknowledge His divine power, and trust the very great and precious promises that He gave us, we will grow in our knowledge and understanding of PTSD, TBI, and compassion fatigue challenges on the home front. As we adjust, plan, and connect, find the right path through this dark place, and work to reengage in community, creatively employing the good God is making from our pain, we must always keep an unobstructed view of our personal Gethsemane. We must always be able to see with eyes of faith that place of refuge that gives us a glimpse of eternity as we deal with invisible wounds of war.

Sometimes forgiveness for ourselves or for those who have hurt us seems impossible to muster. Gut-level fatigue threatens to swallow us whole. When rage finds a voice or a fist, we hurl our desperate cry for help toward the altar before the doors slam shut on our health, our faith, and our hope. Sooner or later, all others fail us, even those in the circle of our most trusted sisterhood. We are inclined to think that God himself has turned His back on us and on our families. Our hearts echo Job's conclusion, "Surely, God, you have worn me out; you have devastated my entire household."[15] The needs on the war-torn home front are full of "hep me, Jesus" times and are too great without God's presence and the comfort of His promises to us.

Jesus Christ is our High Priest who understands our pain. He was tempted in every way but was without sin. He is ready and able to help us.[16] He is our one hope[17] and our healer[18] who alone has the power to restore the injured soul of the warrior and the souls of the warrior's loved ones. Jesus invited the one who doubted to touch His hands and side. The nail prints in His hands and the scar under His heart were wounds of warfare in the ultimate battle He fought for our souls. Jesus said, "Put your finger here; see my hands. Reach out your hand and put it into my side. Stop doubting and believe."[19] His words were an invitation to believe, to trust the only One whose battle wounds can heal those of all others. Jesus extends the same invitation today to scarred warriors and their families: Reach out in faith and touch the Christ who bore in His body on the cross all the casualties we cause one another, both seen and unseen.[20]

As I sat on the edge of Grandmother's bed, I pressed the photo of the Golden Gate close to my heart for the longest time, rocking back and forth in tearful gratitude. Although I did not instantly or even now fully understand all the truths this intersection of heaven and heartache contained, I recognized the sacredness of the moment. From the shadows of His darkest hours, He knew to keep an eye on the goodness of God that was promised to Him.

I tucked the photo into my purse, turned off the lights, and left the house, safe in my Father's arms. And as the screen door swung shut behind me, I thought I heard heaven's congregation erupt in joyful shouts of praise for my renewed strength and hope. Jesus had given me a glimpse of God's faithfulness and my bright future from the foot of His Gethsemane.

Questions for Reflection

1. Do you consider yourself a follower of Jesus Christ?

2. If so, how has your faith in Jesus Christ influenced the way you view your challenges as the family member of a veteran with PTSD and/or TBI?

3. What would you like to say to other family members of warriors about the importance of faith in Jesus Christ in finding strength and victory on the home front?

4. On what biblical truths and Scripture references do you base your comments above?

Epilogue

Post-traumatic stress disorder and traumatic brain injury, the invisible wounds of war, have come home with our loved ones. Though unseen they have the ability to reshape our family dynamics, to restructure our faith in God, and to refine our identity in Christ.

Our journey will have steep climbs, sharp drops, and unexpected turns. Along the way we may experience closed borders, members-only clubs, and clogged spiritual plumbing. Yet if we walk together, we will make it across this demanding stretch of life.

Moses, like all the ancients who were commended for their faith, had a rough path to walk. He "persevered because he saw him who is invisible" (Hebrews 11:27).

Who else could be more qualified to help us with invisible wounds than the invisible God? He has shown us His invisible qualities. "His eternal power and divine nature—have been clearly seen, being understood from what has been made, so that people are without excuse" (Romans 1:20–21). And ultimately He revealed himself to us in Jesus, His Son, who is "the image of the invisible God" (Colossians 1:15).

Our hidden hurts can be transformed for growth and infused with purpose. There is hope and healing for the wounded warrior and for the wounded home when we on the home front fully entrust our invisible wounds to the invisible God.

Now to the King eternal, immortal, invisible, the only God, be honor and glory for ever and ever. Amen (1 Timothy 1:17).

Appendix A

Traumatic Brain Injury and PTSD—What's the Difference?[1]

*T*raumatic brain injury (TBI) is often referred to as the signature wound of the wars in Iraq and Afghanistan. The physical, cognitive, emotional, behavioral, and communicative challenges that follow TBI can have lifelong effects on both the wounded warrior and family members. Many wounded warriors also have posttraumatic stress disorder (PTSD). The combination of a TBI and PTSD create even more complex issues for caregivers and veterans. Very often it is difficult to determine what symptoms, changes, or behaviors are due to TBI or PTSD. It may be useful to complete the following inventory to identify what you are seeing.

Inventory of Symptoms and Consequences after Traumatic Brain Injury

Check areas of change or difficulty that apply to the person who has been injured.

Physical Symptoms—Inventory

- Headaches
- Seizures
- Nausea
- Weakness/paralysis
- Balance
- Clumsiness
- Vision
- Hearing
- Smell or taste
- Appetite
- Sensory sensitivity
- Fatigue
- Sleep disorders

Cognitive Symptoms—Inventory

- Amnesia
- Memory
- Slowed processing
- Organization and planning
- Poor judgment
- Inability to multitask
- Poor initiation
- Confusion
- Easily distracted
- Repetitive thoughts and comments
- Impulsive

Communication—Inventory

- Slurred speech
- Word finding
- Not on topic
- Trouble listening
- Dominates conversations
- Reading
- Writing
- Rate of speech
- Literal
- Comprehension

Emotions and Behaviors—Inventory

- Anxiety
- Depression
- Self-centeredness
- Short temper
- Frustration
- Crying or laughing spells
- Substance abuse
- Mood swings

- Rigidity or stubbornness
- Personality changes
- Dependence
- Disinhibited

Distinguishing between TBI and PTSD

PTSD is considered a mental disorder, but the associated stress can cause physical damage. TBI is a neurological disorder caused by damage to areas of the brain. The major psychological symptoms of PTSD are intrusive thoughts and memories or flashbacks, emotional numbness, avoidance of reminders of trauma, and hypervigilance to possible dangers. When PTSD and TBI coexist, it's often difficult to sort out which condition is causing what behaviors. The following table highlights some characteristics and differences between TBI and PTSD.

TBI	Amnesia—loss of memory for events just before or after brain trauma
PTSD	Flashbacks—intrusive thoughts and memories of the traumatic event
TBI	Sleep disorders—disrupted sleep patterns, i.e., falling asleep, staying asleep, waking early
PTSD	Nightmares and night terrors
TBI	Social isolation—loneliness with loss of friends and support
PTSD	Self-isolation—protective avoidance of situations or reminders
TBI	Flat affect—monotonous or dull speech
PTSD	Emotional numbness—deadened feelings
TBI	Cognitive fatigue—working harder to think and learn
PTSD	Physical fatigue—effects of sleep loss
TBI	Depression—lowered self-esteem, grieving losses
PTSD	Panic attacks—difficulty controlling anxiety
TBI	Passivity—difficulty initiating activity or getting started
PTSD	Hypervigilance—on high alert, can't relax
TBI	Repetition—retells life story to anyone who listens
PTSD	Avoidance—reluctance to talk about war and combat

TBI	Anger—blows up easily when overloaded or frustrated
PTSD	Violence—domestic abuse or use of firearms
TBI	Substance abuse—alcohol increases seizure risks and has intensified effects
PTSD	Substance abuse—alcohol and drugs to self-medicate and block feelings
TBI	Suicide—low incidence in civilians
PTSD	Suicide—higher rates in veterans

Conclusion

TBI and PTSD are complex conditions that require treatment by skilled and experienced professionals.

Appendix B

What Helps and What Hurts

A Word to Civies, Our Civilian Friends and Community, Who Truly Care

*I*n a presentation I share around the country entitled "Fighting PTSD with PTSD," I share suggestions about what the faith community can do to help military families dealing with the invisible wounds of war. I employ the PTSD acronym to help listeners remember what helps and what hurts veterans and their loved ones. Veterans and their families *don't* need

P . . . to be Pigeonholed or Pitied, to be Placated, Pacified, Prodded to share, or Pushed or Preached at

T . . . Trauma caused by ignorance, their Triggers activated, more Temptations to self-medicate

S . . . Surprised or Shocked reactions from us, Sarcasm, taking Sides, or Shame

D . . . to be allowed to stay in Denial, our legalistic Dogma, dry Doctrine

Veterans and their families *do* need

P . . . our Presence, Peace of mind, Professional help, Physical rest, Pardon from real or false guilt, a Plan, a Path, Peers, Pleasure, their Productivity restored, reminders of their Potential, and Provision for material needs

T . . . your Thank-you, simple and sincere, a Team of Trustworthy friends around them, your Time

S . . . your Servant's heart, Solitude, Space to sort it out, Spiritual guidance, Service opportunities, Survival Skills for life Stateside and on the home front, and Side-by-Side interaction (for men) and face-to-face interaction (for women), your Silence vs. clichés

D . . . Debriefing, opportunities to Download memories and questions, a Dream sheet, a map to that Destination, Doors of opportunity

Bridges and Branches

Military life is difficult at best even during times of peace. Military life is *impossible* during times of war without the love and the faithful support of God's people. You may be the bridge who will be used to bring a military member to God and to enable that member and his/her family to bravely answer God's call on their lives.

Military Ministry, a division of Campus Crusade for Christ International, focuses its efforts on the spiritual well-being of troops and their families. Its Bridges to Healing ministry uses a bridge metaphor to help illustrate the role each of us has in the lives of veterans who suffer with PTSD as well as their loved ones and caregivers. Simply, each of us is a bridge, one that makes a physical connection between two others for the purpose of reconciliation or unity. Just as there are many types of bridges that span different kinds of expanse, there are different types of human bridges that span different kinds of needs. Some bridges are gigantic; some are small. All bridges connect and encourage community wellness.

When a nation or group wants to overthrow another group, one tactic in basic military strategy is to take out its bridges and other important inroads. By cutting off its access to fresh provisions or safe exit, a nation or group of people is without resources and without hope. The opposite is also true. In order to save a city, the bridges must be fortified and protected. This ensures that resources will continue to reach those who need them. This tactic saves lives.

What is true for saving cities and nations is also true for preserving people, especially military members and their families. Our ability to remain in the Lord, to stick with the faith, to draw closer to Him is largely a result of the "bridges," the dear friends and family members who were brave enough to connect us with Christ through biblical teaching and persistent intercession, to link us to the Lord, His people and His resources, and to walk alongside us over the deep waters that threaten to swallow us.

Each of us has a responsibility to be a bridge, to connect military members and their families with the relationships and resources available in our communities and nationally that promote healing and wellness. But in order to be an effective bridge, we must remember that we are a *branch*. Jesus said, "I am the vine; you are the branches. If you remain in me and I in you, you will bear much fruit; apart from me you can do nothing."[1] To be effective in helping, serving, or ministry of any type, we must first be filled with the life and power of Jesus Christ and allow that life and power to flow through us to those who need encouragement and solutions.

Appendix C

Additional Resources

Adsit, Chris, Rahnella Adsit, and Marshéle Carter Waddell. *When War Comes Home: Christ-Centered Healing for Wives of Combat Veterans*. Newport News: Military Ministry Press, 2008.

Anderson, Neil T. *The Bondage Breaker*. Eugene: Harvest House, 1990.

Anderson, Neil T. *Victory Over the Darkness: Realizing the Power of Your Identity in Christ*. Ventura: Regal, 1990.

Arthur, Kay. *Lord, Heal My Hurts*. Portland: Multnomah Press, 1988.

Beattie, Melody. *Codependent No More: How to Stop Controlling Others and Start Caring for Yourself*. Center City, MN: Hazelden, 1987.

Beattie, Melody. *The Language of Letting Go: Daily Meditations for Codependents*. Center City, MN: Hazelden, 2003.

Briscoe, Stuart. *Choices for a Lifetime: Determining the Values That Will Shape Your Future*. Wheaton: Tyndale, 1995.

Bruce, Elizabeth J., and Cynthia L. Schultz. *Nonfinite Loss and Grief: A Psychoeducational Approach*. Baltimore: Paul H. Brookes Publishing Company, 2001.

Bubeck, Mark I. *The Adversary: The Christian Versus Demon Activity*. Chicago: Moody Press, 1975.

Bubeck, Mark I. *Overcoming the Adversary: Warfare Praying Against Demon Activity*. Chicago: Moody Press, 1984.

Bubeck, Mark I. *The Adversary at Home: Protecting Your Child From the Evil One*. Colorado Springs: Cook Communications, 1997, 2006.

Bubeck, Mark I. *Preparing for Battle: A Spiritual Warfare Workbook*. Chicago: Moody Press, 1999.

Cloud, Henry, and John Townsend. *Boundaries: When to Say Yes, When to Say No, to Take Control of Your Life*. Grand Rapids: Zondervan, 1992.

Cloud, Henry, and John Townsend. *Safe People*. Grand Rapids: Zondervan, 1995.

Crabb, Larry. *Inside Out*. Colorado Springs: NavPress, 1988.

Crabb, Larry. *Shattered Dreams*. Colorado Springs: Waterbrook Press, 2001.

Croft, Harry A., and Chrys Parker. *I Always Sit with My Back to the Wall: Managing Traumatic Stress and Combat PTSD through the R-E-C-O-V-E-R Approach for Veterans and Families*. San Antonio: Stillpoint Media Services, Balanced Living Communications, 2011.

Dobson, James. *Love Must Be Tough: New Hope for Marriages in Crisis*. Wheaton: Tyndale, 2007.

Doka, Kenneth J., and Joyce Davidson. *Living with Grief When Illness Is Prolonged*, eds. Washington, DC: Hospice Foundation of America: Taylor and Francis, 1997.

Ellis, Albert, and Raymond Chip Tafrate. *How to Control Your Anger Before It Controls You*. Secaucus: Citadel Press, 1997.

Figley, Charles R., and Hamilton I. McCubbin, eds. *Stress and the Family Volume II: Coping with Catastrophe*. New York: Brunner/Mazel, 1983.

Florio, Christine. *Burnout and Compassion Fatigue: A Guide for Mental Health Professionals and Care Givers*. Seattle: CreateSpace, 2010.

Griffin, Emilie. *Wilderness Time: A Guide for Spiritual Retreat*. San Francisco: HarperCollins, 1997.

Grossman, Lt. Col. Dave, and Loren W. Christensen. *On Combat: The Psychology and Physiology of Deadly Conflict in War and in Peace.* Belleville, IL: PPCT Research Publications, 2004.

Hayes, Steven C., Victoria M. Follette, and Marsha M. Linehan, eds. *Mindfulness and Acceptance.* New York: The Guilford Press, 2011.

Horowitz, Mardi J. *Stress Response Syndromes,* 2nd edition. New Jersey: Jason Aronson, Inc., 1986.

Jeremiah, David. *Spiritual Warfare: Terms of Engagement.* San Diego: Turning Point, 2011.

Mace, Nancy L., and Peter V. Rabins. *The 36-Hour Day,* revised edition. Baltimore: Johns Hopkins University Press, 1991.

Markman, Howard J., Scott M. Stanley, and Susan L. Blumberg. *Fighting for Your Marriage,* 3rd edition. San Francisco: Jossey-Bass, 2001.

Markman, Howard J., Scott M. Stanley, Susan L. Blumberg, Natalie H. Jenkins, and Carol Whiteley. *12 Hours to a Great Marriage: A Step-by-Step Guide for Making Love Last.* San Francisco: Jossey-Bass, 2004.

Marshall, Peter. "Keepers of the Springs" from *Mr. Jones, Meet the Master.* New Jersey: Fleming H. Revell, 1949.

Mason, Paul T., and Randi Kreger. *Stop Walking on Eggshells.* Oakland: New Harbinger Publications, 2010.

Norris, Kathleen. *Amazing Grace: A Vocabulary of Faith.* New York: Riverhead Books, 1998.

Remen, Rachel Naomi. *My Grandfather's Blessings.* New York: Riverhead Books, 2000.

Sanders, J. Oswald. *Facing Loneliness.* Grand Rapids: Discovery House Publishers, 1990.

Schutte, Shana. *Betrayed by God?: Making Sense of Your Expectations.* Kansas City: Beacon Hill Press, 2010.

Slone, Laurie B., and Matthew J. M. Friedman. *After the War Zone: A Practical Guide for Returning Troops and Their Families.* Cambridge, MA: Da Capo Press, 2008.

Smith, Patricia. *Healthy Caregiving: A Guide to Recognizing and Managing Compassion Fatigue—Presenters Guide, Level 1.* Seattle: CreateSpace, 2008.

Smith, Patricia. *Healthy Caregiving: A Guide to Recognizing and Managing Compassion Fatigue—Student Guide, Level 1.* Seattle: CreateSpace, 2008.

Smith, Patricia. *To Weep for a Stranger: Compassion Fatigue in Caregiving.* Seattle: CreateSpace, 2009.

Stanley, Scott M. *The Power of Commitment: A Guide to Active, Lifelong Love.* San Francisco: Jossey-Bass, 2005.

Tada, Joni Eareckson, and Stephen Estes. *When God Weeps.* Grand Rapids: Zondervan, 1997.

Tick, Edward. *War and the Soul: Healing Our Nation's Veterans from Post-traumatic Stress Disorder.* Wheaton: Quest Books, 2005.

Waddell, Marshéle Carter. *Hope for the Home Front: Winning the Emotional and Spiritual Battles of a Military Wife.* Birmingham: New Hope Publishers, 2006.

Waddell, Marshéle Carter. *Hope for the Home Front Bible Study.* Birmingham: New Hope Publishers, 2006.

Wiersbe, Warren W. *The Strategy of Satan: How to Detect and Defeat Him.* Carol Stream: Tyndale, 1979.

Wheeler, Joe, ed. *What's So Good About Tough Times? Stories of People Refined by Difficulty.* Colorado Springs: Waterbrook Press, 2001.

Wilson, John P., Matthew J. Friedman, and Jacob D. Lindy, eds. *Treating Psychological Trauma and PTSD.* New York: The Guilford Press, 2001.

Word Ministries. *Prayers That Avail Much.* Tulsa: Harrison House, 1980.

Notes

Introduction

1. "And we know that in all things God works for the good of those who love him, who have been called according to his purpose" (Romans 8:28).

2. Ann Voskamp, *One Thousand Gifts* (Grand Rapids: Zondervan, 2010), 32–33.

3. "Post-traumatic Stress Disorder is the development of characteristic symptoms and responses following exposure to or witnessing of an extreme traumatic event involving actual or threatened death or serious injury to oneself or another. The event results in intense fear, helplessness, or horror. There is the persistent re-experiencing of the event, avoidance and emotional numbing and hyperarousal. The full symptom picture must be present for more than one month and there must be significant distress and impairment in social, occupational or other important areas of functioning. *DSM IV-TR* (Arlington, Virginia: American Psychiatric Association," 2000), 463–468.

4. Patricia A. Resick, Candice M. Morgan, and Kathleen M. Chard, "Cognitive Processing Therapy," Department of Veterans Affairs and the National Center for PTSD, presented at USAF Training Workshop, Wright Patterson AFB, Ohio, 2007.

5. Edward Tick, PhD, *War and the Soul: Healing Our Nation's Veterans from Post-traumatic Stress Disorder* (Wheaton: Quest Books, 2005), 98–99.

6. RAND Corporation. "One in Five Iraq and Afghanistan Veterans Suffer from PTSD or Major Depression," RAND Office of Media Relations Press Release April 17, 2008, http://www.rand.org/news/press/2008/04/17.html.

7. Ken Olsen, "Beyond the Blue Star," *Legion*, September 16, 2010.

8. RAND Corporation study.

9. Tick, *War and the Soul*, 42.

10. John 20:27

11. Chris Adsit, Rahnella Adsit, and Marshéle Carter Waddell, *When War Comes Home* (Newport News: Military Ministry Press, 2008), 8.

Chapter 1: Wounded Warrior, Wounded Home

1. Traumatic brain injury (TBI) is a serious public health problem in the United States. Each year traumatic brain injuries contribute to a substantial number of deaths and cases of permanent disability. Recent data shows that, on average, approximately 1.7 million people sustain a traumatic brain injury annually.

A TBI is caused by a bump, blow, or jolt to the head or a penetrating head injury that disrupts the normal function of the brain. Not all blows or jolts to the head result in a TBI. The severity of a TBI may range from "mild," i.e., a brief change in mental status or consciousness, to "severe," i.e., an extended period of unconsciousness or amnesia after the injury. The majority of TBIs that occur each year are concussions or other forms of mild TBI.

2. Larry Crabb, *Shattered Dreams: God's Unexpected Path to Joy* (Colorado Springs: Waterbrook, 2001), 20–21.

3. Compassion fatigue (also known as a secondary traumatic stress disorder) is a condition characterized by a gradual lessening of compassion over time. It is common among trauma victims and individuals that work directly with trauma victims. It was first diagnosed in nurses in the 1950s. Sufferers can exhibit several symptoms including hopelessness, a decrease in experiences of pleasure, constant stress and anxiety, and a pervasive negative attitude. This can have detrimental effects on individuals, both professionally and personally, including a decrease in productivity, the inability to focus, and the development of new feelings of incompetency and self doubt. American Psychiatric Association: *Diagnostic and Statistical Manual of Mental Disorders,* Fourth Edition, Text Revision (American Psychiatric Association: Washington, DC, 2000), 469.

4. Psalm 17:8

5. Isaiah 40:3–5

Chapter 2: Living Grief: The Pain of the Shattered Dream

1. Elisabeth Kubler-Ross, *On Death and Dying* (New York, Simon & Schuster, 1997).

2. Elizabeth Sikes, article in *The Willing Worker*, September/October 1984.

3. Isaiah 53:3 KJV

4. Hebrews 4:14–16 NKJV

5. Isaiah 61:1–3

6. Ecclesiastes 7:2–4 NIV 1984

7. Henry Cloud and John Townsend, *Making Small Groups Work* (Grand Rapids: Zondervan, 2003), 246–247.

8. Lamentations 3:32

Chapter 3: Dealing with Delays, Detours, and Denied Entry

1. Tick, *War and the Soul*, 141–42.

2. John L. Blehm, Sr. and Karen Blehm, *Angel of Death* (Lincoln: iUniverse, 2008), xix–xx.

3. "All the Rage," *Women's Health*, January/February 2012, 154.

4. Philippians 4:6–7

5. Harriet Lerner, PhD, *The Dance of Anger* (New York: HarperCollins Publishers Inc., 2005), 1.

6. Hebrews 4:14–16

Chapter 4: Smelly Issues and the Fragrance of Forgiveness

1. Ephesians 4:32

2. Matthew 7:3–5

3. John 8:7 NIV 1984

4. 1 John 1:9

5. Colossians 3:13 NIV 1984

6. Luke 1:37 NIV 1984

7. The Parable of the Lost Son, Luke 15:11–32

8. Charles F. Stanley, "Releasing the Offender: The Call to True Forgiveness, 15–Minute Bible Study," *In Touch Magazine*, September 2011, 13.

9. 1 John 2:9–11 NIV 1984

10. 1 John 4:20–21 NIV 1984

11. John 13:12–17

12. Isaiah 30:15

13. Hebrews 13:5

Chapter 5: Weary, Worn Out, and Wondering Why

1. Patricia Smith, Compassion Fatigue Awareness Project, 2012, http://www.compassionfatigue.org/pages/symptoms.html.

2. Ibid.

3. Drawn from Patricia Smith, *Healthy Caregiving: A Guide to Recognizing and Managing Compassion Fatigue—Presenters Guide, Level 1* (Seattle: CreateSpace, 2008), 35–37.

4. Psalm 55:6

5. Job 7:16

6. Ecclesiastes 2:23

7. Smith, http://www.compassionfatigue.org/pages/symptoms.html.

8. John 4:7–14

9. Isaiah 54:5

10. John 4:13–14 THE MESSAGE

Chapter 6: It's His What It Is: Our New Normal

1. Bobby Ghosh, "Looking for the New Baghdad," *Time*, April 3, 2008, http://www.time.com/time/magazine/article/0,9171,1727692,00.html.

2. Psalm 139:16

3. James 1:17

Chapter 7: New from the Inside Out: Breaking the Cycle of Compassion Fatigue

1. Shannon Wexelberg, "Cling," *I Have a Song*, Discovery House Music, 2010, compact disc.

2. Lt. Col. Dave Grossman, lecture, Carlsbad, CA, December 2011.

3. Marshéle Carter Waddell, *Hope for the Home Front Bible Study* (Birmingham: New Hope Publishers, 2006), 36–41.

4. Exodus 20:8–10

5. John 15:1–8

6. We suggest Richard J. Foster's *Life with God: Reading the Bible for Spiritual Transformation* for deepening personal meditation and Precept Ministries International's inductive Bible study method taught by Kay Arthur.

7. 2 Corinthians 5:17

Chapter 8: Faithful Body Parts and the Power of Friendship

1. Adsit, Adsit, and Waddell, *When War Comes Home*, 8.

2. Ephesians 3:17

3. Hebrews 4:16

4. Psalm 68:6

5. Matthew 12:48–50, quoted in Waddell, *Hope for the Home Front*, 124–25.

Chapter 9: Permission to Engage: Spiritual Warfare on the Home Front

1. Vince Lombardi, http://www.brainyquote.com/quotes/quotes/v/vincelomba380768.html, accessed February 28, 2012.

2. Tick, *War and the Soul*, 24.

3. Ephesians 6:12

4. Ephesians 4:20–32

5. Warren Wiersbe, *The Strategy of Satan* (Wheaton: Tyndale House Publishers, 1979), 36.

6. Hebrews 4:12

7. Adsit, Adsit, and Waddell, *When War Comes Home,* 148.

8. www.biblestudytools.com.

9. Galatians 5:20; Revelation 9:21; 18:23; 21:8; 22:15.

10. John 10:10.

11. Mark I. Bubeck, DMin, "Re: Spiritual Warfare and PTSD . . . a few more questions," January 14, 2012, personal email.

12. Daniel 10

13. DSM-IV-TR, 631.

14. Neil T. Anderson, *The Steps to Freedom in Christ* (Ventura: Gospel Light, 2004).[[Is there a page number for this quote?]]

15. Luke 10:19

16. Wiersbe, *The Strategy of Satan,* x–xi.

17. John 10:10

Chapter 10: The Savior's War Wounds: Our Hope

1. Hebrews 4:14–16

2. Isaiah 53:3

3. Romans 8:28–29

4. Matthew 3:17

5. Mark 10:38

6. Philippians 3:10–11

7. Luke 21:37

8. Luke 24:50–51; Mark 16:19

9. Zechariah 14:4

10. Luke 22:46

11. Mark 16:15–18

12. Isaiah 53:5

13. 1 Peter 2:24

14. Esther 4:14

15. Job 16:7

16. Hebrews 4:14–16

17. Ephesians 4:4
18. Isaiah 53:4–6
19. John 20:27
20. Adsit, Adsit, and Waddell, *When War Comes Home,* 8.

Appendix A: Traumatic Brain Injury and PTSD—What's the Difference?

1. Source: Lash, Marilyn (2011). Lash and Associates Publishing/Training, Inc., Youngsville, NC, www.lapublishing.com.

Appendix B: What Helps and What Hurts: A Word to Civies, Our Civilian Friends and Community, Who Truly Care

1. John 15:5

Marshéle Carter Waddell served with her husband, CDR (ret) Mark Waddell, a career U.S. Navy SEAL, for twenty-eight years around the world. Her first two books, *Hope for the Home Front: Winning the Emotional and Spiritual Battles of a Military Wife* and its companion Bible study, *Hope for the Home Front Bible Study* (New Hope Publishers 2006), arm other military wives with God's promises of His presence, power, and protection. Together with their three children, the Waddells have endured many lengthy separations and frequent deployments for combat duty, special operations training, and real world conflicts for more than two decades. Today, her husband is a disabled combat veteran with PTSD and multiple TBIs. Her son recently returned from his second combat tour with Operation Enduring Freedom, Afghanistan, with the 3-7 U.S. Marines.

Marshéle is an international speaker for military, government, and women's events. She is the founder and president of Hope for the Home Front, a nonprofit 501c3 corporation, based in Fort Worth, Texas. She was awarded the Bloomberg Assistantship at the University of North Carolina at Chapel Hill and is currently pursuing her MA in Journalism-Strategic Corporate Communication.

Kelly K. Orr, PhD, ABPP, is a USMC Vietnam veteran with more than thirty years of experience in clinical psychology, behavioral medicine, and pain management. He reentered military service with the Air Force in 1987 and retired in 2004 with a combined active duty Marine Corps and Air Force career of 25 years.

Dr. Orr serves on the advisory council and speaking team of Hope for the Home Front and has led a training workshop on PTSD with Campus Crusade for Christ's Post-Traumatic Stress Disorder ministry, Bridges to Healing. He continues his work as a behavioral medicine consultant with family medicine clinics, churches, and a national healthcare facility development company.

Hope
for the
Home
Front

Many of our returning veterans have experienced combat trauma and are suffering with the pain and confusion of Post-Traumatic Stress Disorder (PTSD) and Traumatic Brain Injury (TBI). Their wives, mothers, daughters, and loved ones are deeply impacted by their war experiences. Hope for the Home Front serves to fortify **ALL WOMEN** connected to a wounded combat veteran of any conflict by providing them with resources, books, seminars, weekend retreats, and community connections. We educate, encourage, and empower these women to find hope, healing, and solutions for themselves and for their families so that they may not only survive the aftermath of war, but thrive on the home front.

If you or a loved one would like to find support, please visit
HopeForTheHomeFront.com
WoundedWarriorWoundedHome.com

Or email **info@hopeforthehomefront.com**